War on Waste Innovation

Leonard Bertain, Ph.D.

Leonard Bertain, Ph.D.

War on Waste Innovation

Encyclopedia of:
Terms, Phrases
and Concepts

Leonard Bertain, Ph.D.

CEO University Press

Oakland, California

iii

Leonard Bertain, Ph.D.

Additional copies of this book may be obtained
from your local bookstore or the publisher:
CEO University Press
3758 Grand Avenue, Suite 25
Oakland, CA 94610
510-653-6355

For more information on the concepts and processes described in this book
please contact: **The Bertain Group**
3758 Grand Avenue, Suite 25
Oakland, CA 94610
Tel: (510) 653-6355
drelbie@pacbell.net

To my business friends,
Who have helped me stay focused.

Len.

Leonard Bertain, Ph.D.

Introduction.

Over the last 25 years, I have been telling people about my work in delivering the War on Waste and the role of Tribal Knowledge in the program. Unfortunately, I use "terms, phrases and concepts" that are crystal clear to me but are not always been entirely obvious to my interested listeners.

It turns out that we have evolved over a hundred terms, phrases and concepts that are unique to our view of business. And so I would like to explain as best I can what these terms all mean in our context of a business innovation system.

Mind you, we didn't invent all of the terms. We have just put our own spin on them. And this spin has been able to help the CEOs that we work with to manage their companies with our philosophy of business. As a result of this work, many of our client companies have made big improvements in their profits. We have also noticed that some of our clients (roughly 20%) have made not just big but "dramatic" improvements in their businesses. And we call these companies "Quantum Leap Companies."

It is not sufficient to merely make this observation. We want to know "why" the Quantum Leaps occurred. We think we know why and so we are reporting our findings in this and a number of books in this "War on Waste Book Series."

Len Bertain
Oakland, CA
March 2014

Foreword

Our consulting practice focuses on the public sector market. When I first heard about the War on Waste, I was intrigued. We all hear about the inefficiencies of government organizations and how they abuse the fiduciary and fiscal responsibilities that they have been trusted to manage. I wanted to know more.

When I first talked to Len Bertain, his description of the War on Waste and the role of Tribal Knowledge in its delivery was a logical way for our consulting business, Canal Bridge Consulting, to bring a message to these organizations. And I think it is a message that they want to understand. And the message is this, "there are inefficiencies everywhere. (Len's War on Waste has been directed at over 150 companies). Not just in government agencies. And believe it or not, we can use some of the same techniques that have been applied to manufacturing and other industries to reduce the cost of government."

I was consulting in the Washington, D.C. area when the previous administration developed the idea of reinventing government. The War on Waste is targeted to do just that. All the methodologies are there and they will work in government.

I look forward to making the War on Waste an effective methodology for our clients. It will benefit them and all of us who support the Public Sector with our taxes.

Susan Stalick, President
Canal Bridge Consulting
Bethesda, MD

Leonard Bertain, Ph.D.

War on Waste Innovation

Table of Contents

War on Waste Innovation

The War on Waste

The role that Tribal Knowledge plays in the War on Waste (WOW) is the focus of this book. We have evolved a set of terms that we use when we talk about these processes. HVLC Ideas are those that are High Value (HV) in their benefit to the company and Low Cost (LC) to implement. We define Waste as "anything that doesn't add value." The objective of both WOW and HVLC Ideas is the same: to take High Value opportunities involving Waste and coming up with LC or Low Cost solutions. We learn a lot about a company's strategy when we do this. So when you read this section pay attention to how that happens.

Leonard Bertain, Ph.D.

Tribal Knowledge

Tribal Knowledge is the collective wisdom of the organization. It is the sum of all the knowledge. It is the knowledge used to deliver, to support, or to develop value for customers. But it is also all the knowledge that is wrong, imprecise, and useless. It is knowledge of the informal power structure and process or how things really work and how they ought to. It is knowledge of who constrains the process and who facilitates it. It is the knowledge that is squirreled away by employees who feel a need to protect their jobs by not sharing the information needed to do a job. This is part of the totality of the Tribal Knowledge.

For example, it is the knowledge and the experience of the assembler who won't tell others how he can put those two casings together (when no one else can). That knowledge is his job security. But more importantly, it is the untapped knowledge that remains unused or abused.

We spend a lot of time with employees in the War on Waste getting to know a company's Tribal Knowledge. We don't really ask employees to tell us all they know. We go about it in a different way. We get them to talk about their work (because that is where the Tribal Knowledge is) and boy do they talk. The vast majority of employees love their companies. After all they get paid to work there. But more importantly, they spend 40 plus hours a week there and grow to make good friends.

So when we go into a company and start asking about how they do things, in the framework of our War on Waste, people are ready to contribute. The funny thing is that people rarely look at the knowledge that they have accumulated as very valuable to the company, except maybe the guy above who

2

squirrels away key pieces of information to give himself job security.

As we go through this book, you will be exposed to a whole bunch of stuff that contributes to how we both learn about the Tribal Knowledge and how we make sure everyone is aware of others in the company that have valuable information to help solve a problem. In context, almost everyone wants to help a company get better and that is what we talk about in this book. Tribal Knowledge Innovation is all about using that vast resource of information that employees have that makes a company tick and ultimately, keep on ticking.

The War on Waste

We start the book by going back to the basics. Just what is waste?

We use Henry Ford as a source because he was the inspiration for the Toyota Production System (TPS). In the Henry Ford world, assuming for a moment that a corporation should be a waste-free environment, there would be no accountants, no order entry clerks, no purchasing people, no managers, no desks for salesmen, and so on. Why?

Because Mr. Ford believed that these functions and activities were not value adding. In other words, Henry Ford only wanted manufacturing jobs (those that added value) and he practically detested all the other jobs needed to run the administrative and support functions of his business.

When I stood in front of a group of people and declared a War on Waste, I got push back from the accountants. They were a waste but a necessary one.

I began to call them, "necessary waste." They didn't like that either. So I changed my tune and looked at the glass as being "half full" and elected to call them "essential support" as noted in the figure (below).

The 3 Activities of an Organization

They are "essential" only if they support the adding of value. Accountants do something that is useful as support for those doing value-added work. This is why the administrative side of the business can generate so much waste.

They don't do value-adding things. And they often lose sight of that fact. They may support the delivery of value but they don't "add value."

So what we do in the War on Waste program is to help teams identify waste and support them as they figure out high value and low cost (HVLC) solutions.

When we started the War on Waste in 1985, the Toyota Production System (TPS) was getting a lot of attention. It was the foundation of the phenomenal success of Toyota in car production quality and efficiency.

Taiichi Ohno, the developer of the TPS, identified 7 major wastes (or in his terms – muda):

War on Waste Innovation

- **Waste of over production** (largest waste) – making too much of a product and not being able to sell it. Idle finished inventory or WIP is a big waste.

- **Waste of time on hand (waiting)** – of course this would be waste because while a worker is not adding value, he or she is costing the company money.

- **Waste of transportation** – while products are moving from building to building or around the factory floor, no value is being added to them. This is a big waste.

- **Waste of processing itself** – when Taiichi Ohno looked at many of Toyota processes, he found that they were not very efficient in delivering value. They were very wasteful. The changeover of dies was a big waste that translated into time waste. Ohno's engineer Shigeo Shingo figured out a very clever way to efficiently manage the set-up of dies during a changeover. He was able to reduce set-up of dies from 24 hours to less than 10 minutes. That was a big deal.

- **Waste of stock at hand** – if you have stock in inventory waiting for production that is a big waste. It ties up cash. So the concept of Just in Time (JIT) evolved to make sure that inventory was managed to arrive at a factory just in time to be used in the manufacturing process.

- **Waste of movement** – whenever you look at a factory and see a worker or a pallet of materials moving around a factory, that is a waste. People can't add value walking around, and material can't have value added to it if it is moving around the factory.

- **Waste of making defective products** – this is almost obvious, but it was the foundation of the thinking of Total Quality Management (TQM) a number of years ago. Phil

Crosby and a number of quality gurus became phenomenal successes by focusing their efforts on reducing quality defects. This has, in turn, led to the current 6-Sigma craze.

These are all well and good but…they don't cover all the areas of waste in a business. They certainly can be guides for how a piece of paper moves through an office. If it waits at any stage, it is a waste of movement. If a worker has a pile of work at her desk and the others in the office have no pile of work, maybe there is an imbalance of work in the process.

All of these things have been part of our War on Waste history. And people, if given the chance, will find these problems.

So we put our own list together because there are a whole bunch of things that aren't on the Toyota Production System (TPS) list of wastes.

Here is a caution: Don't get hung up on how people categorize waste. That distracts their effort. These categories are only meant to give guides to teams working on a project. They may have a waste that is similar to one of those noted and when they see it, it just might trigger another way to look at their problem.

Our improvement process is straightforward. If you get employees to look at the parts of your operation that are wasteful, they will usually get into one of the following areas (a little different way to look at waste than in the TPS):

Time - Anyone who does anything or any process that wastes time. This is usually the easiest to find.

Inventory - Raw material, work-in-process or finished goods. When you fix a waste here, it goes right to the bottom line. This was one of the original TPS wastes, but we make sure that people think of inventory in all stages of production.

- scrap/rework/seconds

Logistics - the movement of finished goods to your customers or raw materials from your suppliers. When you work on logistics, you touch all the shipping and delivery companies that deliver or ship materials to or from your facility.

Lost sales opportunities – this is totally ignored by TPS. There are all kinds of inefficiencies in the way you take orders, failure to have materials on hand that the customers need in a distribution business, and so forth.

You also get into issues here when you miss opportunities because your product is close but not close enough to meet customer's needs. Maybe it needs an upgrade and no Executive is willing to make a commitment to get it done.

Waste in products offered – We have had a lot of fun with this issue over the years. Here are some of the issues that have come up:

- Poorly designed products – they are hard to repair, they break, or they don't work when taken out of the box.

- Over/under specified products and services.

- Poor quality – just like in TPS.

- Long delivery lead-time – this is a big waste if you are 50% longer than your competitors. This is a fun waste to get into because there are all kinds of root causes of the production problem causing the long lead-time.

- Non-responsive to customer needs – this usually costs a company a lot of money in lost sales. If you fail to deliver what the market wants, that is a big waste.

- Misdirected marketing & sales efforts – this applies to two departments: sales and marketing. The problem here is that lots of wasted time is spent trying to sell the wrong product to a customer or having a marketing campaign that is inappropriate. You can see how far the War on Waste can reach when you start to get into marketing and sales.

- Slow/inactive inventory – this is a killer waste because all the slow moving or inactive inventory is just plain waste. It is costly to a company. In many cases, management just doesn't want to deal with it.

- Promised delivery failures – boy this is a big waste in lost sales. How many dollars of lost sales are found here?

- Slow attention to customers – if you don't care to take care of customers you might as well fold up the tent. I once had a client who was not attentive to their customers, late for 90% of the orders. One of the employees, of less than sterling character, said that he was surprised that they had any customers. The CEO jumped into action because if this guy thought they were bad, they were bad.

- Wrong product for the market.

- GAP between customers' view of company and company's view of company.

- Missed customer intelligence opportunity

War on Waste Innovation

IT Networks – In more recent years, IT finds its way into our analyses because of the waste of aging technology in support requirements (cost to fix), speed of network response, and most importantly support staff requirements.

Waste of Capital

- Inventory (raw/WIP/finished)
- Under-utilized floor space, equipment and facilities
- Wrong application of company cash.

Logistics

- Warehousing of supplies & finished goods
- Physical distribution & freight

Support Services

- Sales, admin, management and engineering functions

Advertising Waste

- Target audience wrong
- Selling wrong benefits
- Contradictory messages
- Unfulfilled promises
- Inconsistent messages
- Wrong messages
- Wrong media
- Under spending/overspending
- Projecting wrong image

Leonard Bertain, Ph.D.

Other resources - utilities, facilities and equipment, out of pocket services.

Inappropriate Moment of Truth

I have included this one as a way to address hotel workers and others in hospitality. A Moment of Truth is an encounter between a customer and a business.

This can be in person, over the telephone, over the Internet or any other way business is transacted. Each such encounter leads to a "Moment of Truth." And the experience can be either good or bad, as Jan Carlzon, former CEO of SAS Airlines, noted in his book, "Moments of Truth."[1]

There were over 50,000 encounters with customers at his airline when every passenger or phone call contact is defined as a Moment of Truth. He reasoned that since he couldn't be present for every MOT, his company had to be totally customer focused. He trained his people to be prepared to help customers.

Lead Time Waste – This could be included with wastes in Cycle Time as well. But I included it as a separate waste because I recently had a fun engagement around this issue. The company CEO asked me to focus the various teams on projects that would reduce lead-time.

It was fun because I had never done a war on waste quite like that before. We completed the project and they have reduced the lead-time. It has gotten everyone on the same page.

As we have learned, waste is everywhere in an organization and as you begin to dig into the War on Waste you will find

---

1. Carlzon, Jan "Moments of Truth - MOT" Harper and Row, New York, 1987

10

War on Waste Innovation

opportunities abound to fix what we call the low hanging fruit. Even if you don't elect to change to the Quantum Leap Company, the War on Waste is a great way to analyze your business. We make it a little game. We tell people we want them to find $100,000 in annual waste that can be fixed for a total expenditure of less than $2,000.

Now that's a game with some meat on it.

We get employees to find opportunities for waste elimination with a benefit to cost of 50 to 1. That's a 5000% ROI. And it leads to process improvement and profit creation. This is a great way to change the company. Let me remind you that our approach to business improvement is based upon listening and acting on the ideas of these employees. We get them to move ideas from the suggestion stage to actual implementation and measurement.

All of that has worked at each of our clients. In one two year period, we delivered the War on Waste to 26 clients. The benefit to them was $28 Million in savings with costs of implementation of projects of $735,000. A 3800% rate of return isn't bad. (Please see the accompanying chart)

These numbers are very interesting. These numbers come from real work with real companies. These numbers were audited by the State of California. They are very real. Looking at the chart, note the shaded numbers. These numbers tell us that from 23 companies (actually it was 26 companies with three line items in the chart actually being two companies with a single owner combined as one) the War on Waste program generated $28 Million in savings on ideas whose total cost of implementation and validation of the savings was $735,000. As the figure in the lower right tells us that we achieved an average ROI (return on investment) of 3805%. People tell me that that is pretty good. Another analysis has shown a net profit improvement of over $400 Million for the first 3 years at 50 companies involved in our War on Waste program.

CLIENT	Number Trained	Number of Ideas	Number of Projects	Annual Savings First Year	Solution Cost	ROI in First Year
Manufacturers						
Tools and dies	39	93	10	$1,391,675	$61,029	2280%
Commercial signs	13	57	3	$358,000	$5,725	6253%
Food processing machinery	10	61	13	$205,750	$6,275	3279%
Plastics forming business	14	91	33	$201,100	$1,690	11899%
Grinding shop	29	204	38	$812,045	$113,353	716%
Steel forging company	28	152	12	$517,356	$22,017	2350%
Electronics parts	32	101	8	$722,250	$81,038	891%
Printing plates	33	71	12	$1,445,109	$9,980	14480%
Injection molded plastic	50	262	16	$2,260,301	$16,075	14061%
Fireplace accessories	39	87	18	$347,119	$11,830	2934%
Distributors						
Aluminum supplier	23	79	19	$144,660	$11,695	1237%
Faucets and accessories	33	104	12	$906,423	$23,361	3880%
Computer distributor	47	151	8	$4,645,250	$40,000	11613%
Computer distributor	38	85	6	$1,137,231	$14,200	8009%
Computer distributor	22	52	4	$1,121,085	$15,372	7293%
Truck parts distributor	37	104	65	$2,287,100	$60,392	3787%
Building materials	60	131	12	$2,116,300	$79,834	2651%
Building supplies	79	385	21	$2,331,652	$46,473	5017%
Barbecue accessories	34	76	16	$191,790	$1,900	10094%
Produce distributor	41	263	8	$1,260,726	$18,232	6915%
Service Companies						
Repair and service of valves	44	202	27	$1,058,408	$80,675	1312%
Diaper laundry service	19	65	4	$795,000	$7,970	9975%
Programming services	42	92	6	$1,746,625	$6,825	25592%
Totals	806	2968	371	**$28,002,955**	$735,941	
Averages	35	129	16	$1,217,520	$31,997	**3805%**

If you look at the chart a little more carefully you see that the worst ROI was around 800%. That tells you that if you set your expectations on following our prescription for changing your business that you should expect to see $8 back for every $1 invested but you also see that the average is $38 of profit for every $1 invested. There are a number of people that we can talk to in the investment community that would give you all the money in the world for that type of return.

12

War on Waste Innovation

No Blame

The War on Waste (waste is anything in the company that keeps money from being made) begins with an idea (see "Idea").

It doesn't matter the size of the company, if you want to find out what's wrong with the company, listen to an employee's idea. The idea is not just any idea; it is an idea that identifies a waste in one of the business processes.

In our definition, the War on Waste is a company-wide affair. Everyone participates. And all parts of the company are open to review. No part is spared. It is one of those times that it is OK to pass judgment on the inefficiencies of a neighboring department. The War on Waste methodology brings teams together of different work groups to look for waste. It guides these project teams on how to analyze a waste by finding out how much inefficiency it contributes to the company in actual dollars. In fact, we believe so strongly in this concept that we trademarked "No Blame." The trademark symbol is intended to symbolize to our clients and their employees that we are going to drive change at their company and we do it by invoking "No Blame." It is change without reprisal.

Leonard Bertain, Ph.D.

The initial focus begins with "No Blame". No Blame is at the root of this methodology that has been developed to insure that all suggestions for improvement have a chance to get a fair hearing. We don't want to blame anyone for a problem. We want to find out "why", "what", "when", "where" and "how" but we don't care about "who". If we want to solve a problem or improve a process, we can't blame people for creating the problem. We just need to fix it.

People want to help. They are willing to help. But they aren't going to help if it means that they are going to lose their job. This is a concern at all of the companies that we have delivered the War on Waste. People are insecure about offering ideas if their manager or foreman is going to make their life miserable. So the idea of "No Blame," or no reprisal, allows these folks to venture up to the table of risk and offer suggestions to eliminate waste. And when they are rewarded and praised for their ideas, boy is that ever exciting!

Perhaps the most important thing that can be pointed out about No Blame is this: the idea is the root of any change and NO BLAME protects the idea. This is like the freedom of speech. Without the freedom for people to assemble to listen to your free speech, free speech is neutered. No Blame then is to an idea, what freedom to assembly is to free speech. The US Bill of Rights was framed with a very simple understanding of what was necessary to insure a free democracy. The Bill of Rights lays down the law very clearly on the relationship of free speech to freedom of assembly. One of the problems with the Chinese dilemma at Tiananmen Square was that the Chinese were touting that they had free speech and when someone began to exercise their newly found power, it was abruptly curtailed by forbidding "freedom of assembly." So in our view, if you want to improve a business, if it needs to change, then ideas are necessary and ideas are protected in our approach with No Blame.

Ideas

John Steinbeck once said, "An idea is a solitary moment."[2] If you think about that it probably is true but when an idea is shared with others a good idea can grow to become a great idea. We encourage the sharing of ideas in the War on Waste for precisely that reason. But ideas don't survive in most companies because there are obstacles in the way. We have discussed some of those obstacles in the segment on Black Knights. Black Knights are idea "obstructers." They get in the way of ideas.

We trademarked No Blame to make sure that all ideas had a chance to get a hearing. No Blame gives someone with an idea enough courage to step forward and put it on the table for consideration. I like to think of myself as an "idea protector." If anyone gets in the way of an idea during the War on Waste, our facilitators are there to insure that the idea is given consideration. We are particularly on the alert for the Black Knights and others who want to stifle an idea before it has a chance to get some support or at a minimum some consideration.

In our recent experience, we have found a way to approach the negative aspects of our dealings with Black Knights. When we thought about it, we could almost guarantee a fight with at least one company Black Knight. In a large corporation, they were everywhere. And it wasn't a fair fight because we always won over the long haul because we didn't fight with them unless the CEO agreed to support us.

---

[2] Steinbeck, John *East of Eden* Penguin Books, 1986 p. 170

Leonard Bertain, Ph.D.

I guess my feisty nature made the challenge a fun one. But our goal wasn't to engage Black Knights; it was to help the company become more profitable. And so, we changed our tact.

We realized that helping employees achieve respect in their work was a nobler quest than fighting Black Knights. During the War on Waste, we helped employees gain earned respect and that was the premium achievement. But we wanted to neutralize the Black Knights and make innovation and improvement of Tribal Knowledge part of the culture of the company. And we could do that if we trained Executives and Managers alike to include improvement of Tribal Knowledge as a touchstone of the company's management paradigm. I am going to discuss this in more detail throughout this book but my business associate, George Sibbald and I are going to cover it in more detail in a soon to be released book entitled "The Tribal Knowledge Paradigm." This change of management is different but it guides managers and executives to look at their primary jobs as twofold: managing to improve profits and acknowledging improvements in Tribal Knowledge as it aligns with company Mission.

This new paradigm encourages learning. We know that the process of learning involves students asking questions, getting answers and testing the depth of their knowledge with new ideas. Whether this learning environment is a workplace or a primary school, new ideas or questions need to be treated as sacred. If an idea comes up, it must be respected. That is integral to the Tribal Knowledge Paradigm. So during the War on Waste, we set up the Tribal Knowledge Council to be the point of entry of ideas (any ideas) in a company. And we set it up so that it reports to the CEO. The reason for this is that this gives everyone the understanding that ideas are important and in a learning corporation ideas are to be respected and protected.

Black Knights

We have spent a bit of time talking about the Black Knights. They are the people in any organization who interfere with the implementation of ideas. They are usually those in the organization that don't want change. For them, they have a nice little life that change will disrupt.

We got the idea from the Monty Python movie, "In Search of the Holy Grail." There is a scene in which the Black Knight is defending a bridge against another knight who wants to cross the bridge. Of course, the Black Knight wins, "he always wins."

As King Arthur approaches, he asks to cross the bridge. The Black Knight refuses and a battle begins with swords clashing and ultimately the Black Knight loses one arm, "It is but a scratch", then the other arm and then both of his legs.

As he sits there, the Black Knight is a stump of his former self, King Arthur calls it a draw and moves on across the bridge.

Why is this funny? Well, the bridge is over a small creek and King Arthur could just as well have jumped across the creek and continued on his way. But he doesn't. He must cross that bridge!

So a couple of things are going on. The Black Knight is defending a stupid position, the bridge across a creek. And King Arthur challenges him, probably unnecessarily.

I enjoyed this scene because I had seen it just after I had an encounter with a Black Knight in a small business. He ended up defending the status quo and the CEO told him emphatically that they were going forward with the great idea that an employee had suggested. The CEO had not lopped off his arms and legs yet but he almost got to that point. Of course, the CEO prevailed and from that point forward our use of this analogy has been an integral part of the War on Waste.

In a typical engagement, I might show the Black Knight scene from "In Search of the Holy Grail." (You can view it on YouTube.) And I might say something like, "most companies have a few of these people hanging around." And then I might ask something like, "do you have any of these people here?" And boy do I get laughs and lots of people looking around the room and mouthing a name or two.

But, as I noted in the previous section, we are trying to get along better with Black Knights and we have discovered a way to do that in the Tribal Knowledge Paradigm. In fact, it is through our encounters with Black Knights that our solution to a better paradigm emerged. After all, we need to give them an alternative management option. The proposed option will allow them to save face and join the team.

Change without reprisal

This is what War on Waste is all about. If you want to make your organization receptive to change, there can be no reprisal (getting even) on people who offer suggestions for improvement. You must protect those ideas for change with No Blame. It is "No Blame Change." And it is the foundation of the Tribal Knowledge Paradigm.

In one of my early engagements, a worker was really excited about an idea that he had. He went home on the first weekend of the War on Waste and drew up a precise engineering rendering of his solution. He was not an engineer. He was a line worker in a factory. When he got to work on Monday, he was very excited. He gave his papers to the foreman who was just throwing out the coffee grounds for the first pot. The foreman looked at the papers and then dropped them into the garbage can followed by the grounds.

The poor employee grabbed his papers from the garbage can and ran over to me. He was angry and afraid. He was angry that his hard work was dismissed so casually. And he was afraid that the foreman was going to do something to him. Of course, the foreman tried but we were able to protect our employee's idea and turn it into a success. It was a wonderful idea that cost about $100 to implement and increased the output of his work area by 15% ($250,000 increase output per year). John Steinbeck's may have said it best:[3]

> "...And this I believe: that the free, exploring mind of the individual human is the most valuable thing in the world. And this I would fight for: the freedom of the mind to take any direction it wishes, undirected...and this I must fight against: any idea, religion, or government *or corporation* (the authors words) which limits or destroys the individual. This is what I am and what I am about."

I won't get into what I did but it was not nice. After all, that foreman had just thrown the gauntlet down. Believe me, I was up to the challenge. You don't do that to anyone. You don't. Ideas must be accompanied without an attitude of reprisal of any sort. And as leaders, we must fight to protect those with the ideas.

No Excuses

The No Blame motto was developed to encourage employees to come up with ideas. It serves as their protection from the Black Knights that fight change in the organization. But there is a downside. When an employee invokes "No

---

[3] Steinbeck, John *East of Eden* Penguin Books, 1986 p. 171

Blame" there is no accountability and that's why we came up with the idea of "No Excuses".

When an employee team fails to measure up to its capabilities, they accept the consequences and report the data honestly. They do so with the understanding that "No Blame" is the operating philosophy of the company. And that is what we want. However, a manager has the right to investigate the reason for the low performance under the banner of "No Excuses." In other words, the workers use "No Blame" and the managers invoke "No Excuses." We call this "accountability."

An interesting note here is Silicon Valley executive, T. J. Rogers, who leads with No Excuses in his management and holds people accountable to a rather stern management approach. There is no shield with No Blame.

I don't necessarily agree that that is a good way to manage. But his results are most impressive.

Mabel

Mabel is an important person in the evolution of War on Waste. The story began twenty-five years ago, as I stood in front of a group of employees who had been forced to attend a class I had been contracted to deliver. It was a training

War on Waste Innovation

program that introduced a small manufacturing company to the principles of the Toyota Production System (TPS). In essence, I was teaching a method for identifying and eliminating waste in business processes. To illustrate my thoughts about how this system should be applied to American industry, I had prepared over 160 slides, including charts, graphs, illustrations, text and checklists. I was to show these slides in conjunction with a series of interactive lectures scheduled to run for ten weeks at the rate of three one-hour sessions per week. As with all of my projects, the entire company was required to attend—everyone from the custodial personnel to the CEO.

On this first day of class I had a rude awakening. I introduced myself and moved right into my presentation, feeling pretty good about the way things were going. I was on the fourth slide and I noticed a raised hand at the back of the room. "Yes?" I said, wondering what could be confusing this early in the presentation. After all, this was the great Len Bertain in front of her.

"My name is Mabel," she said, "and I have a problem." Mabel was a middle-aged production worker who'd labored on the assembly line for over twenty years. "I can't understand your slides," she said. I asked her why not, expecting a smart-assed answer and thinking wearily to myself that there was always one in every group. Her answer astounded me: "I can't read," she said.

So I tried to clarify what she had said, "do you mean you can't see my slides clearly?"

"No," she said, "I am illiterate. I can't read."

I was blown away. The whole four months' worth of material I had prepared would be of no value to her—nor to anyone else that couldn't read. I had assumed reading was a basic skill, forgetting that some production and line workers don't have much more than an elementary-school education. Yet they all needed to learn the skills outlined in this new management system.

How would I keep Mabel up to speed with the rest of the class? I didn't want to single her out any more than she already was. Yet it was imperative that I communicate to this class in a way the rest of the classes would find compelling and appropriate. I had very little time to decide: forty pairs of eyes rested on me, waiting for my next move.

And the War on Waste emerged.

I appealed to their individualism by opening up the lecture to the employees and posing a question: did they know of any wasteful processes currently in place at the company? My question was greeted with hearty laughter: talking about how messed up the company is has to be every employee's favorite pastime. But before the conversation could deteriorate into a negative, company-bashing free-for-all—because that's what it was quickly becoming—I outlined a few rules. I call this "chalking the field" which is defining the boundaries of the discussion.

We would identify a wasteful process and make an early attempt at finding the root cause of the problem. I told them not to worry about what anyone else would think about the idea and not to blame anyone for the inefficient process in place. I wanted them to concentrate on thinking of the best way to solve the problem. The removal of blame allowed the full force of employee individualism: when you identify a waste, you experience the strength of individual thinking. And because Mabel spoke English and had ideas, she became involved in the process.

War on Waste Innovation

Hands shot up faster than I could call on people. People from every corner of the room were sharing their thoughts about things that just weren't working right in the company:

- Poor lighting in the production area caused workers to make mistakes.
- Disorganized machine tools and fixtures wasted a lot of time.
- Inventory not there when it is needed for an assembly wasted more time.
- Poorly designed packaging wasted employee time because all four sides of the packing boxes took a long time to tape.
- Expensive Styrofoam coffee cups were used in the coffee room.

The list developed over a couple of days until we had about forty-five different items to think about for this group. I listed each item on a flip chart, using pictures and simple diagrams whenever possible.

I was thrilled by the enthusiasm I was seeing. All the ideas weren't big money makers but the enthusiasm was intoxicating. While I always tried to make my lectures interesting, I'd never experienced participation on this level. But it made perfect sense: these people spent their lives in the trenches, working with these inefficient processes day after day until I imagined some of them wanted to scream out of sheer frustration. They'd never before been asked to voice their opinions. Now, finally, someone was asking *them* what was wrong with the company. What a rush!

And Mabel was the impetus for the War on Waste methodology that evolved.

Added value (or value-added)

There are a number of ways to define this term. We define it simply as "what customers are willing to pay for." In any business, everyone needs to understand why the business exists and how it makes money. As we do the War on Waste, we ask a very simple question, "What does this company do to add value?" The answer to this simple question serves as the basis for the War on Waste.

So the question "what is waste" is intimately tied to the company's value-added activity. There is an interesting thing that happens in the War on Waste. As employees start to identify waste, they are reflecting the effectiveness of a company's ability to deliver value. All those things that occur in a company that keep the value from being added efficiently are wastes. During the War on Waste, we look at a company's value-added proposition very closely. And the process for doing that is very thorough.

What we have found out is that very few employees of companies have any clue as to what the company does to add value. When we ask a typical employee of a machine shop, "What does this company do to add-value?" it is amazing that most of them have never thought about it. After a few minutes of discussion, someone notes that it is obvious that a machine shop makes money only one-way: when chips are being produced. But then some wise guy asks if they are adding value when they do assemblies for their customers. Of course, they do. Customers are paying a small fee for the assembly. And then one of the ladies in the quality department asks "what about our military customers that also pay to inspect their parts?"

In some of our earlier work with companies, I would walk into a company with a simple business and no one could tell me what they did to add value. What do the customers pay for? Gradually they are able to see the correlation between the term "added value" and "what they do for customers" and "what customers will pay for." I remember having a very

War on Waste Innovation

interesting discussion with employees over 25 years ago at a small bank serving the needs of high profile executives.

When I asked, "what is it that you do to add value?" The room was silent. Of course, people put their money in the bank and expect a number of services to be provided. But, for instance, what is the added value part of the loan processing service? That may be clear to anyone reading this book but it wasn't to those in the room. So, "who does the added value work in processing a loan?" This was a very important question. Once we knew who added value, we could then determine what the "right work" of the bank should be.

We use the term "right work" as contrasted with "working right" because if you are delivering value and the wrong work is being done right, then that still is a waste. If you do the "right work" but do it wrong, that is also a waste. So when we analyzed the added value of the bank, we analyzed the current workflow and found out that the wrong work was being done. For instance, when a loan was initiated for a wealthy individual, the loan documents were put in a folder. And as the folder passed through the various clerks and administrators at the bank, it went serially from desk to desk. Why? Why couldn't it go in a parallel fashion to those who had a need to know and serially to the key document-signers? "It's required by Federal Law to do it that way!" Whenever I hear something like that, the red cape of challenge has gone up and I charge.

So the first thing we did was find the "Federal Law" that said this. Of course, there was none. When we went to the Chairman of the Board to explain our problem, he was really surprised that someone had introduced the Federal Government into the equation unnecessarily. But they had done that over 20 years earlier. Once we found out that there was no governing Federal Law that said "how" records should be processed, we had gotten to the root cause of the issue. We could now define the "right work". And we did. But we needed to determine the optimum flow for the signatures. We did that.

One of the neat problems that we solved to increase the processing speed of the loan was this. These loan documents started before all the papers were in. Usually the individual's tax documents were the last in. So when we got all the documents but these tax papers, we started processing the loan documents. We even got the loan committee to pre-approve the loan pending acceptable tax records. So when these last papers hit the bank, it was on red-alert. These were bankers ready to "rock and roll." They were able to tell their clients that if they got all their documents in the door, they could have their loan papers ready to sign the next day. In fact, in most cases, they could do so within 3 or 4 hours. They developed a neat little "red alert" system. It went something like this.

When the last document hit the bank, it was placed in a "Red Folder." The Red Folder was now on "Red Alert." If the red folder hit your desk, anyone in the company could alert you to that fact, wherever you were. In fact, the Red Folder put everyone in the company on alert that the final loan papers were in house ready for approval of the loan.

This example points out a couple of interesting points about the term "value-added". First, once employees know that value-added has something to do with how the company makes money, they can then get involved in looking at the company's inefficiencies in doing so. That is what the War on Waste is about.

A second point is that very few companies are clear about all the ways that they make money and how these different ways are tied to strategy. In the definition of strategy, as per Michael Porter, it is any number of value-propositions. A

War on Waste Innovation

value-proposition is a statement of what a company does to make money or a statement of how it adds value. The interesting part of this logic is that the War on Waste is intricately tied to an analysis of the effectiveness of the company strategy. If the implementations of the various value propositions or the added value activities are flawed, then the strategy is flawed. This is exciting stuff to think about because if you work at a company and you think you know the strategy, then go down to the lowest working person in the company and see if you can determine whether there is a correlation between what the workers are doing and the defined strategy. And a more important issue, do the workers know the company strategy? As a thought to consider, in the example at the bank, how did the War on Waste help align the company's strategy with process?

Matsushita, Konosucke[4]

A number of years ago, I ran into this quote from Konosucke Matsushita, the founder of Matsushita Electric in Japan. This quote served as my initial call to action in literally all War on Waste projects from 1988. His quote:

> "We will win and you will lose," he says. "You cannot do anything about it because your failure is an internal disease. Your companies are based on Taylor's[5] principles. Worse, your heads are Taylorized too. You firmly believe that sound management means executives on one side and workers on the other; on one-side men who think and on the other side men who can only work. For you, management is the art of smoothly transferring the executives' ideas to the workers hands.

---

[4] Manufacturing Engineering – February 1988

[5] Editor's note: Frederick Winslow Taylor (1856-1915) propagated the principles of "Scientific Management" in industry and business. He was Henry Ford's time and motion expert.

Leonard Bertain, Ph.D.

"We have passed the Taylor stage. We are aware that business has become terribly complex. Survival is very uncertain in an environment increasingly filled with risk, the unexpected, and competition. Therefore, a company must have the constant commitment of the minds of all of its employees to survive. For us, management is the entire work force's intellectual commitment at the service of the company... without self-imposed functional or class barriers.

"We have measured–better than you–the technological and economic challenges. We know that the intelligence of a few technocrats-even very bright ones-has become totally inadequate to face these challenges. Only the intellects of all employees can permit a company to live with the ups and downs and the requirements of its new environment. Yes, we will win and you will lose. For you are not able to rid your minds of the obsolete Taylorisms that we never had."

Think about it. Is he still right?

Common Cause

One of the early observations about the War on Waste process was that it got employees to rally around what we call a "common cause." Serving on a project team during the War on Waste amounts to finding a waste and eliminating it with a CEO-approved solution. The project team rallies around a project that becomes the team's common cause. We have observed that successful project teams need to be clear about their common cause in order to be successful. Our reason for pushing teams to rally around their project is that, otherwise, the spirit of individualism takes over and chaos ensues. If an individual on a team has an idea and is willing to work with others on the team to improve the idea, then the team has a chance to succeed.

The common cause is the part of a team's "raison d'etre"

28

that is missed in many tomes written about creating teams. Without the common cause, the team doesn't exist. Barry Bonds was endowed with powerful individual talents as a baseball player. But even he knew, that given certain situations, he might have to take a pitch in a given situation that would improve the chance of winning.

Fortunately, most individuals are delighted to collaborate on a realistic plan of action that will allow a team to win. And that is what the common cause is all about. It defines how a team will win.

And we make the common cause even easier to identify. We tell employees that they have to quantify a waste of at least $100,000 and can't spend more than $2,000 to fix the problem. This gives everyone a clear goal. They have to work together to figure out how the identified problem causes waste in the company and quantify these things in hard dollars. And then they need to figure out a solution that doesn't cost a lot of money. And that sometimes takes a lot of thought. But the fun thing, there have been over 10,000 teams that have done this before, so it isn't impossible.

Discovery

Discovery is the process that a team will go through as it tries to understand why a particular problem exists. It involves trying to reach the root cause of the problem. It is a search to discover "what's so" in a company. In particular, the Black Knights must be managed during the discovery stage of the War on Waste because the process challenges them, their base of control, and their existence. So during the discovery, each team should:

- Challenge important ideas and conclusions.

Leonard Bertain, Ph.D.

- Pose incisive questions and design special observations or experiments to obtain definitive answers.

- Explore unexpected or puzzling events as opportunities.

- Put effort and capability into creating adequate test methods.

- Scrutinize information for bias.

- Evaluate the validity of the measurements.

- As the uncertainties arise, the process requires that the problem-solving teams resolve these uncertainties.

- Leave room for doubt: Do not stifle it.

- Recognize and acknowledge ignorance;

- Decide what is unknown, or poorly known, that would be valuable if known.

- Decide what information is needed and how to get it.

- The facilitator must guide the teams in testing facts and ideas. Clearly we want new ideas, but the facilitator has certain rules to follow:

  o Be clear about the rules for converting data to "fact".

  o Check offered "facts" for evidence and validity.

  o Test hypotheses of solutions using common sense where possible.

These are all part of the process of improving Tribal Knowledge. They serve as foundations for the managers and executives who are supervising the process of improving Tribal Knowledge. If they fully understand the above, they will be doing OK.

The CEO's Job

We found out a lot about the CEO's job when we did all those War on Waste initiatives over the last 25 years. We learned that the CEO has to be in charge of change. We also found that the CEO needs to manage innovation because that is the source of new products and lots of money from Internal Growth. And finally, and most importantly, we found that the CEO needs to continually drive to improve Tribal Knowledge. We used to think this was done as serial initiatives but realized that it needs to be a constant flow, not a discrete event. And he needs to train his management team to do likewise. It is through this continual infusion of management energy that is the foundation of the Tribal Knowledge Paradigm. This section gives the reader a good deal of insight into these issues.

Leonard Bertain, Ph.D.

Culture

A simple definition for culture: "The principles established to guide employees in performing the responsibilities entrusted to them." The culture reflects the personality of the organization and the shared beliefs that determine how its people behave and solve business problems. The culture lays down the guiding principles of the company.

The "company values" are the ethics that guide decisions. The "culture" is the style of how we live and survive in the daily operation of the business. A culture may change as it evolves over time, but its values should not.

Herb Kelleher defined a clear culture for Southwest Airlines. I know that I like to fly Southwest Airlines because the employees are really committed to the culture and values of the company. They all seem to be enjoying their jobs. They like working there. And the culture should do that. It should give employees a clear view of what the company expects of them as employees as well as what you should expect from the company.

I have a client that has evolved a special culture. He is a unique character and his culture reflects that. He loves to work late and of course he comes in late. But he expects all of his employees to come in on time. When I first got there, I tried to change him. He couldn't be changed, so I did. I had to recognize that his employees and everyone around him created a culture that reflected his unique behavior. It even applied to the way he did engineering.

For instance, one project had an engineer who was modifying a piece of production equipment to improve its capacity. The modifications required lots of input from the owner. The engineer would go home for the evening and the owner would come in and make a change in some feature of the equipment. Most of the time, changes were documented, sometimes they weren't. It was really a weird environment. He was a mettlesome owner. But when I asked the engineer about this, he said, "You know how he is." I sure did. But his business managed to survive and the end result was a culture that reflected his unique behavior. I wouldn't recommend working in his culture because it was very difficult. But his employees were very loyal to him.

My point with this story is this; Southwest and GE both have very logical and understandable cultures. In GE's case, it evolved over the years from Thomas Edison. I am sure Edison had his own quirks and I am sure that they reflected on the early culture at GE. Herb Kelleher certainly laid his mark on Southwest Airlines and Jack Welch has his influence on the GE culture of today. But as I work with the wide range of companies as I have, it becomes clear the odd characters as noted above, can and do create cultures that manage to survive. And sometimes it is a wonder.

Agenda

One day while I was waiting in the foyer, a client walked in fuming: "The son of a bitch is still here. I thought we buried him 18 years ago." And he stormed off.

I like this kind of stuff and I was intrigued. I knew something about the company history. The father had died and had left his two adult sons the responsibility of running the business. Neither of the boys was really ready to run the business, but they did and had so far survived reasonably well.

Had the father suddenly "materialized?" Obviously, he had done some damage. His spirit was apparently still around and causing trouble.

Leonard Bertain, Ph.D.

What had actually happened over the years was that, while they had learned enough about running the business, their key foremen and managers resisted any changes. They always wanted to run the business the way the "Old Man" had run it. They resisted any new ideas. These managers weren't insubordinate, the new CEO and his brother were just not clear about their agenda. The managers and foremen knew that if they simply waited long enough, the idea behind the change would fall by the wayside and the "old way" would return.

The "burial of Dad" was a painful process, in more ways than one. Dad was a good guy, and he had managed with a strong hand. Everyone knew Dad was in control. When he died, his sons took over the *ownership* but did not take *control* of the company. They hadn't established their own approach to running the business and they had not defined an agenda for themselves. For sure, the son who became the CEO did not have his own agenda, and he was not in control.

As a CEO, you must have an agenda. An agenda is nothing but a list of things to do. It is like the meeting agenda. Every meeting should have a list of issues to be discussed. Everyone attending the meeting needs to know where it is going and what items are going to be discussed. The agenda for the CEO is no different. It is the list of what he/she wants to do while CEO.

The difference, of course, between a meeting agenda and the CEO's agenda is that the meeting agenda is common knowledge to all participants at the meeting. However, the CEO's agenda is usually secret. And well it should be. Parts of the agenda that needs to be executed or implemented by others may be shared, but the grand plan is best kept a guarded secret. And it should be noted that as necessary as an agenda is, and even how important it is to keep it secret, it should not be etched in concrete.

As a CEO gets more and more familiar with the job of being CEO, the agenda can change. For instance, a CEO may set as an agenda item a goal to create an organization that is driven to perform above all the businesses in the industry - to create the Quantum Leap Organization (See definition under Page 118). It isn't easy, and may require discipline that the CEO may not possess. There are coaches available in the form of corporate mentors, YPO or Vistage type associations, or consultants. On top of all this, the CEO needs to develop a plan that incorporates this agenda item into the grand plan. There are a number of techniques to integrate agenda items into business plans. The CEO may wish to get more sophisticated in management ideas and may elect to attend an Executive Training Program as a way to execute a particular agenda.

Once the agenda is defined, certain things will fall in place. In the vignette above, where the sons taking over the business after the father died, the CEO did not have a clearly defined agenda. He did not know what he really wanted to accomplish. His word should have been sufficient to cause things to move in the direction he wished. But he couldn't make it happen. His managers weren't clear what he really wanted to do. They just knew that if he wanted to change anything, they wanted to resist it.

So what does this CEO do? Does he fire the managers? Does he put them on report until they toe the line?

This isn't about change. This is about, who is in charge. The foremen didn't believe the son of their "leader" was able to lead the company. But they felt that they could. "Just watch me!" was their refrain. In this case, the son's agenda would need to be very simple: Get control of the company. This would not be easy because the problem managers had been their father's right hand guys and had watched the boys grow up. It is hard to give up control to someone you knew as a little kid some 20 years earlier!

In our view, the agenda is the CEO's life list. It is the things that s/he wants to do as CEO and in a private life. How you go about this is your choice. We have worked CEO's through their life agenda and it is fun to watch the action unfold. It is almost like magic. But it doesn't happen without the list.

Who's in Charge Analysis

This is pretty simple. The CEO is in charge. And don't forget that. If you are trying to bring some democracy to your organization be very careful. A typical corporation is not a democracy and some painful, unilateral decisions have to be made. A well-run company more closely resembles a benevolent dictatorship. When decisions are made there is no vote. The CEO makes the critical decisions.

One of my pet peeves with various CEO's that I have worked with involves any decision that they make to change the company structure. It is not a decision that is open for management vote.

For example, Lean Manufacturing is one such change process. Conceptually, it is a wonderful idea. In practice, it was a grandiose failure. And I think there is a simple reason for that: the CEO's of those company's who tried to change to the new paradigm demanded by TQM didn't understand that they had to lead the change. It is the CEO's responsibility to lead any paradigm change or any paradigm shift.

As we will explain in more detail in the book on the Tribal Knowledge Paradigm, new initiatives are wonderful. They serve as a way to infuse a burst of energy into a company and good things come from that infusion of energy (sometimes). A better approach is to use any of those energy infusion initiatives to kick-start a program that recognizes the value of Tribal Knowledge improvement and then leaves the company with a management paradigm that supports that approach. Improving Tribal Knowledge should then become part of the management paradigm.

Strategy

Strategy is probably the most misunderstood part of the CEO's job. Let's begin with a definition. Michael Porter, the great Harvard University strategy guru, defines strategy to be "any number of unique value-propositions."[6] And a "value proposition is any number of ways to make money." The value proposition is the same as the "value-added" concept that we use when we define waste. The strategy of a business defines the activities that will be used to create the "unique set of value propositions."

This serves as a lead-in to what happens in the War on Waste. We help everyone to get clear about our definition of waste. In the War on Waste, waste is defined as anything that doesn't add value. To make this definition palatable to those in a company that don't add value (payroll clerks, AR and AP clerks, shipping clerks, CFO's, etc.), we have defined an activity called "essential support" to single out jobs that are necessary but not value-added. So in WOW, we get very clear about the "value proposition" because that is how waste is identified. If employees are crystal clear about the value delivered by the company, then they will be able to identify

---

6 "What is Strategy?" by Michael Porter, Harvard Business Review, and Nov-Dec 1996 - reprint number 96608.

waste. So we target all projects to look at waste. In a way then, these projects reflect the success of the CEO in being able to execute strategy. If the strategy is good, but the transference to employees is not, it should appear as waste.

For example, if a metal fabricating business has a defined strategy to be a JIT supplier and their machine set-ups are higher than the industry averages, then it won't be able to deliver cost-effective small batch runs demanded by JIT. The wastes identified in the WOW class will almost always find this. Because the strategy is targeted at JIT, one of the ways of making it work is to have small batch sizes. In JIT factories, you never want any production active with inventory that will not be consumed by a customer within days. In the JIT world, inventory has got to move quickly from production to the customer's production facility and out the door to their customers. And so we see in this example, that the War on Waste has aligned the company strategy of being a JIT Supplier with their process of shorter set-up times for the machine tools. I think that this is a significant consequence of most WOW projects. We have helped to align strategy with process.

Another example of strategy disconnect or "waste" might be the strategic commitment of management to deliver all products in 2 days and the average ship time is actually 3 days. This is "strategic lip service" at its best. So in the War on Waste at this company, excessive lead-time will be addressed. That is a guarantee. Employees hear the CEO and managers saying that they want 2-day shipment but they don't do those things necessary to make it happen. This is fertile ground for the War on Waste. If delivering product isn't happening, you can guarantee that employees will zero in on that and more than likely, there will be a number of different projects addressing various aspects of this problem. Lawrence Bossidy,

War on Waste Innovation

the former CEO of Allied Signal made this aspect of the War on Waste very clear when he said, "at the end of the day, I don't bet on strategy, I bet on people." And that is exactly what we do in the War on Waste world, "we bet on the people."

Michael Porter is also very fond of saying, "When you are competing on operational effectiveness, it's very hard to sustain an advantage, because everybody, of course, tries to imitate your success." So isn't the War on Waste an operational effectiveness based idea? Yeah, it is. But in order to be able to compete successfully you just may need to improve your operational effectiveness. At that point, you may have defined a strategic advantage in which case you have used "operational effectiveness (OE)" to gain a strategic advantage. It isn't a sin to use OE as a strategy but Porter is right on. Once you have shifted from being market niche follower to a dominant market niche leader, people will imitate your success. So when you become the market leader, you have a whole new set of problems to worry about.

This point has raised a number of issues with various CEOs. Granted, at any moment in a market niche, there will be a leader and followers. The goal of course it that once you become an industry market niche leader, you want to stay there. And of course that is hard to do. Brad Mattson, CEO and founder of Mattson Technology made an interesting observation here. His company had been fighting to become the industry leader in their market niche. Once they got there, they realized that they were vulnerable because their strategy had been designed to compete as a follower. So they modified their strategy and started acting like the industry leader. At any moment in time, the swap from leader to follower is going to go on. And your strategy will change accordingly. Or you may stay the course that got you there. Whatever, strategy is not stagnant and it must be etched in Jell-O not granite. It must be subject to review and critique in an ongoing basis.

Consider this example. A client had found that during the War on Waste his machine shop was able to deliver parts to his main client on a very efficient Just in Time fashion. We had developed a Kan Ban system (a self-scheduling parts management system) to manage his inventory. But he also got so good at running the quoting process that he could quote a part, produce a sample and deliver it with the quote. This became a component of his new strategy. Now he was worming his way into the customer's engineering pool and he became the preferred vendor for pilot run samples needed by engineers. They just didn't want the hassle of working with anyone else. In this way, he became a part of the engineering staff and his people knew about opportunities long before his competitors. So he used the Operational Efficiencies to gain competitive advantage, but as Michael Porter points out, he knew others would emulate his success. And they tried. He used the results of the War on Waste to change the rules of the competition for business. He was now the industry leader and had to continually set new rules for competition that others would have to emulate.

That is what strategy is all about. In his case, the machine shop owner had whole range of Operational Efficiency improvements that he was going to use to his strategic advantage. It turns out, that he had six years of success maintaining an edge on his competition using operational efficiency advantages. But one of the interesting aspects of this discussion is that he realized that he needed to get into doing assemblies for his client. This was good business because he got more margins on the assembled units. By continuing to react to his customers' requirements, he used his efficient production shop to extract more value from his customers. And all of these benefits began with the War on Waste effort targeted at machine set-up reduction.

The reason that this example is good is that it shows the progress of a company from the War on Waste to Strategy changes to New Visions for the business. The CEO was very sensitive to the changes in his company vision that resulted from these business improvements. His initial vision was that he was a "quality machine shop." As he became more efficient, his vision was that of "an efficient just in time supplier of parts." And it evolved to become a "major partner to semi-conductor equipment manufacturers from idea to production." The CEO of this story stayed right on top of both his vision and strategy.

WOW and Strategy

We observed that there is a very real link between WOW and major strategy change in just about every one our engagements. It was not immediately clear to us why this happened.

Then we went back to the basics of WOW. It starts with understanding what value-added means. Then we look at waste as anything that doesn't add value to the product process. But how this related to strategy required a major link and that came from Michael Porter's[7] treatise on Strategy in which he defines strategy as any number of value-propositions.

So when you go back here you find the following logic: the waste is anything in the process that is not value-added and WOW is the program that looks at this; strategy is the value-added proposition to the market; and so, WOW looks at the efficacy of strategy from the bottom of the organization.

---

[7] Op Cit - Michael Porter is the Harvard University guru on Strategy.

So what does this mean?

For one, looking at where value-added products or services are being delivered monitors strategy. This is not our normal concept of how you run a business and track strategy. It is almost counter intuitive. It says that by keeping the monitoring of strategy in the hands of the super-educated MBAs, you are missing the boat.

In other words, if you want a successful strategy, you need to involve those on the front lines of where the value-added service or product is being delivered or created.

I have a subtitle in my book "The Tribal Knowledge Paradox" that reads like this: **"Using the War on Waste to align Strategy with Process."**

And that is a major thing of what WOW is about.

View

A view is what you see. In War on Waste words, the view of a CEO is what he sees in his customers, suppliers, employees, and business processes. And the view is a two-way exchange. If the customer has a different view (a negative one) of the company, then the CEO cannot have a clear view. The CEO with a foggy view of customers may not see all the untapped business opportunities and may miss opportunities to participate with the customer in new product designs that competitors are locking up.

A friend of mine, Niel Klein, showed me a neat way to look at this. His theory is that when you introduce a new product, it is an "article of faith." There is no guarantee that anyone will want it. Surveys can help poll the market but prior to launch, the new product is an intangible. It is a series of assumptions that you believe (not know) that you can sell profitably to someone else. In this frame of reference, your products and services are defined by the perceptions of your customers.

Customer Perception

	Low	High	
Internal Company Perception	FOOLS PARADISE	HEAVEN ON EARTH	High
	HELL ON EARTH	CANCER WITHIN	Low

In the box above, ideally your customers and company staff will have high perceptions of your product or service. If you follow the figure, you see that life is miserable for any business when both the customers and the company's internal personnel have a negative or low opinion of the product. So when you take simple surveys and they show you squarely in the "Hell on Earth" area, you need to do something. You have to accept the numbers and do something about them. It is a time when reporting honest data with No Blame is critical. The bold leader does these little surveys because they are usually accurate and can very often save a company from a dramatic catastrophe in quarterly earnings. But haste is absolutely a must.

To avoid these negative situations, if CEOs just took time to look, they would see the possibility of generating another 30% in sales by spending time with the current customers and understanding what they want, or where suppliers need to be to win more business. The CEO needs to get out and talk to those top 5% of customers who account for 67% of the revenues (the 5/67 customers). In the New Economy, if you don't have a clear view, you will lose these key customers.

If you ask a CEO about his top 10 customers and try to get an accurate assessment of how they are doing, the customers typically have one view and the CEO another which leads to a survey with results in the lower left quadrant. In one War on Waste project, the CEO was quite pleased with a 90% on-time shipment to his customers. Since his top 10% customers accounted for 87% of his business, they were guaranteed to have at least one late shipment each week. This CEO did not have a clear view that matched his top customers' expectations.

One of the employees, the janitor, was shocked when he learned about their on-time record. He couldn't understand how they could have any customers if they didn't ship orders on time. The CEO was disturbed when this particular employee made that comment. The employee had a less that sterling character with his off work activity. He wasn't mad at the employee; he just realized that if this person thought it was bad, it really was bad. Within the framework of War on Waste, the CEO didn't bite the employee's head off for speaking up. The employee spoke his mind and it hit home.

Most CEO's have one view of their employees before they begin the War on Waste. But that view can change. Recall Mark Twain's comment: "When I was 17, my father was not a very smart man. It was amazing how much he learned over the four years when I finally returned home at 21." In fact, most employees don't change during the War on Waste as much as the CEO does. The major benefit of the process is that both CEO and employee can engage in problem solving based on each one's increased awareness of the other's value to the company

War on Waste Innovation

One particular CEO in our experiment was a very bright guy. It was rarely necessary to say anything twice. He really "got it" even though he is a highly educated MBA (sic!). One day he was complaining about how slow everyone was in getting things done. As luck would have it, he was giving directions to one of the employees, and it was obvious that his instructions weren't precise. On top of that, he was dealing with a Russian immigrant whose English was only passable. As the communication progressed, it was clear that the programmer was going to run off and write what he thought he had been instructed to do—different from the instructions he was being given. It was a disaster in the making.

I intervened and suggested to the young President to take some time, write down a functional specification of what he wanted from the engineer and then review it with him before the engineer started writing a computer program. Although this appeared to be a slowing down process, he could also see the value of this exercise. He knew that if he didn't do this, lots of information would be lost in the communication and the time to complete the project would be extended.

So what does this story tell us? As a CEO or company executive, you need to be aware that you can create a clear view of your employees and business processes if you focus on open communications based on No Blame concepts. If the CEO had blamed his engineer for not being expert enough with English, he would have failed at getting his directive accomplished. The clear view is a two-way exchange.

Another client had a large inventory that wasn't turning over rapidly enough. The physical size of the fundamental inventory units meant that significant square footage was going to be needed to store all the material. In the War on Waste class, the employees designed some neat shelf storage ideas.

But none of them was as good as the idea (which wasn't new) to go to the supplier and work a deal to give him a larger commitment of raw material. If the supplier kept this raw material on his shelves, the company wouldn't need as many shelves on their premises. This idea was not new but the CEO's foggy view of the supplier kept this option from view.

In the discussion, the supplier agreed to take back some of the unused raw material which freed up the shop floor storage space. An agreement to increase the commitment of raw material was signed, and a weekly delivery of needed raw material was defined. Both sides won.

So when the supplier view is discussed, think about how that relationship can work differently. One of the strategies for Zero Working Capital creation is to reduce inventory or to increase inventory turns while at the same time implementing a Just-in-Time Inventory system. You can't make these kinds of improvements without a clear view of your supplier, and this clarity is readily achieved during the War on Waste.

Vision

One definition of vision is a point of view about a likely and a desired future of the industry. It might be a perception of how the organization will function in this projected future. It would look at the company's focus, strategies, value, culture, competitive position and its competitive advantages.

Another dictionary defines vision as: "the ability to perceive something not actually visible." The CEO has to be able to create the vision for the company. S/he needs to have a clear view of the business and move it to a higher plane to create a vision. The CEO needs to look at the market, at the current customers, suppliers, and partners, and at employees and business processes. If the view is not clear, s/he will create a vision that is a pipe dream and not a possibility. The ideal vision for a company is one that looks into the future, and the employees and everyone involved should be able to see that the vision defined by the CEO is attainable. It may be a stretch, but it is attainable.

There aren't many CEOs who run their businesses with a clear vision. One CEO, however, who manages a small manufacturing division of a very large manufacturing conglomerate, has a crystal clear view of the customer, suppliers, employees and business processes. He keeps all activities of the business focused on achieving his vision for the company. He knows that his vision is a stretch of the company capabilities but it is achievable with a strong focus. His vision is very simply, to be the company that "customers will come to because we deliver rapidly against their aggressive requirements." And his method of focusing everyone is "We will achieve our vision by improving all of our internal processes by reducing product cycle time. All process improvements will lead to an increase in revenue per employee."

This guy has it. His vision has worked its way into everyone's thinking about what to do next. It becomes easy to decide which projects had the highest priority by their consistency to this vision statement. It's simple. If a project would reduce cycle time but it required more people to do the job, it probably wasn't as likely to get funded as a project that recommended a reduction of cycle time and reduced the number of people needed to do a job. The concept is clear to the employees. Employees know that when they have an idea to buy a piece of equipment, its cost must be justified based on productivity improvement.

Leonard Bertain, Ph.D.

Chalking the Field

When I was growing up, my family lived in the country and we had a field that the neighboring farm kids and I would use to play baseball. We didn't have chalked lines to mark the field but we had things just as good. We had the old Redwood tree that was a dead totem out in one of the farmer's fields and we had the edge of the barn. That was the first base line. The third base line was the fence post and the tree in the corner of the field.

Of course, home, first, second and third bases were cow pies. Not fresh ones of course. So when we played a game, things went pretty smooth until a questionable foul ball got everyone in a tither and issues arose. Eventually, the issue was resolved and the game continued.

I mention this as the foundation to what I call "Chalking the Field" because when my kids were playing baseball in the totally organized life of the city kid, they needed chalked fields to play baseball. If I were to take them to an empty field, they would not be creative initially but they would have figured out how to "Chalk the Field" on their own if they wanted to play a game. If you don't have chalked lines you have to agree on a different approach and they would have come up with the same things we did many years earlier. They did that because they needed boundaries and rules to play the game. What was a fair ball? Who calls strikes? And so forth.

We do a similar thing in a business. There are rules that define each job. But there aren't necessarily rules to define how the game of winning at the company will be played. Jobs are isolated and metrics applied to the tasks involved. But when you have a group of people working to a common goal of optimized output of the group, they are a team and the rules that define winning need to be made clear. The rules amount

48

to "Chalking the Field." And that is what I mean by this expression.

If the General Manager or the COO or even the CEO wants to get optimum results, they need to engage the team members in a discussion of the work rules for a winning team. Of course, they can dictate that but that usually gets sub-optimal results. Or you can just let the people try to put the rules together without any guidance from management and that is another prospect for a failure. It should be a management/worker effort. So the person responsible for the end result is recommended to be part of the "Chalking of the Field" team.

And don't forget that you need to keep score. Everyone on the team needs to agree on when a run is scored and when an out occurs. These simple understandings lead to very positive work because no one wants to play a game where the score is not kept or they don't know if they are winning or not. And the score should be posted at the end of the game (daily) so that every one knows how they did in a particular day.

I like my "yes/no" charts (yes or no if something happened) because they are simple and let people know if they won very quickly. For instance, if a team's goal is zero defects, then at the end of the day, the manager or supervisor can put up a "yes/no" chart with a simple question, "Did we work without a defect today?" If the answer is no, you put a big red "X" on the chart as soon as the defect is detected. If at quitting time, there is no red "X" on the chart, then a green "O" goes up to indicate no defects. (see page 67 and following for more detail on Yes/No Charts)

People have complained to me that they didn't like that chart because it put a lot of pressure on them to not let down the team members. I usually would say something like "duh, that's what it's all about." By keeping everyone focused on performing flawlessly for a whole day, is tough. So then you start to figure out ways to make it easier and that is what WOW tries to do. Once they see that it is possible to deliver defect free products, the employees get excited that they can achieve that goal. It may have been a stretch but they put the metrics down and see progress with the goal in sight. That is fun to watch.

Eating Crow

My definition: the act of having to admit to the world that you were wrong. In War on Waste, it doesn't make any difference. We don't even care that you made a mistake. We have a motto that we use in our CEO training institute, CEO University, which guides us here "actio – eruditio – confectio" (act – learn – adjust). It serves us well in guiding CEOs. Don't worry about eating crow. Eating crow is all about worrying about being wrong. The War on Waste is all about getting it right without blame. The CEO's of most businesses have to be in control and if they make a mistake, they are not in control.

For a CEO who managed a company in the previous environment before the Tribal Knowledge Paradigm, the output management philosophy of the War on Waste, eating crow was unheard of. It wasn't the macho thing to do. As CEO's begin a War on Waste project, they find that the training process is very tough on them. One of the better CEOs said that he found the War on Waste difficult because when I made him eat crow, I didn't provide catsup. I never asked him to eat crow. I never ask any CEO to eat crow, I just ask them to listen to employee ideas, act on them with respect and when something goes wrong, it isn't the end of the world. Just fix the problem, don't blame anyone and get on with it. If they want to eat crow, give them catsup.

War on Waste Innovation

Management After the Fact

In a conversation with Ray Dolby of Dolby Laboratories, San Francisco, CA, he pointed out an interesting aspect of his management style that has infiltrated the Dolby culture. Ray has a number of interesting approaches to management. One of them, he terms "Management After the Fact." It is Ray's belief that in his industry a Sales organization has to act with a sense of urgency. So when a Sales Person or anyone in the company sends a quote out to a customer, he requires that all such correspondence be made available in a file that he looks at every day. So if a salesman sends a quote out and s/he is a bit too generous with Ray's money, Ray will see the quote and "after the fact" discuss the deal with the responsible person. He calls this "Management after the Fact" because he wants people to move with a sense of urgency to get quotes out the door. If problems arise, then he is able to deal with it "after the fact."

One of the issues that Ray took with me during our discussion was the concept of "No Blame." He said that "Management after the Fact" is looking for guilty parties so that their problems can be corrected. In my early comments, I had made the point that No Blame was not concerned with who created the problem. Ray objected because he said that he wants to know who created the problem so that he can correct it with "Management after the Fact." No Blame is about holding people accountable. That's where No Excuses comes into the discussion. If you work in the No Blame environment you will be accountable for your actions. The War on Waste CEO will demand No Excuses while the employee invokes No Blame. In Ray Dolby's case, the employee who needs to be corrected after the fact knows that Ray is interested in educating the employee about the proper way to send a quote

51

to a customer or the proper way to write a proposal or how to price the offer. But Ray is also smart enough to know from his experiences that if you get into the process of holding up quotes before they leave the company, the sales cycle will be dramatically impeded. In Sales, you want a sense of urgency. And so he doesn't get in the way before the proposal goes out, he does it "after the fact."

As an aside, the "day folder" that contains this sales correspondence has an attendant folder that contains copies of all incoming purchase orders. This is important because anyone who has an interest in the new sales orders can interject ideas into the "purchase order process" to insure that orders are processed correctly. For instance, a sales person may receive a purchase order from a customer and misinterpret the intent of the customer. An interested engineer who knows the customer and who reads the daily purchase order folder will find the error, correct it with the Sales Person and thereby, reduce the probability of delivering the wrong order to the customer.

A side value of the purchase order file is that employees are able to see whom they are getting orders from. It is exciting to realize the range of customers that put orders in to Dolby Laboratories from Disney Studios to Sony.

CEO Calculus

One day I was playing golf with a former client who had successfully managed to sell his business for significant personal gain. He deserved it - he had not only worked hard but he had worked smart. He made an interesting observation. He said, "If I were ever to run another business, I would spend my time working on the value-added part of the business and leave the accounting and other administrative functions to accountants and the arithmetic crowd. I would work on the calculus..." In his words, this was "CEO Calculus."

War on Waste Innovation

I thought about this a lot. He was really saying: Don't get sucked into the details. Work the broad picture. Don't lose your vision. Others can do the arithmetic: the accounting, the presenting of charts on output. The job of the CEO is to engineer the business with problem-solving skills, and a vision about where the business should be going. The CEO should be building the bridge using his "CEO Calculus" so that employees can move to the next level of performance.

And that is not accomplished in the Board Room. It is accomplished by seeing the execution of strategy first hand and by knowing that "the bridge" that he creates will support the organization. The CEO needs to spend his/her time focusing on the part of the business that delivers value to the customers. The value-adders of the organization are those responsible for providing the products or services that customers buy. They do the value adding.

My client's reason for spending time with the value-adders had very simple logic: cost accounting and other administrative functions only deal with reduction of overhead and cost containment issues. The value-added part of the business allows you to increase the margins, improve return internal growth and reduce working capital ratios. By focusing on the value-added part of the business, it is possible to improve cycle times of products, reduce lead times, monitor the execution of strategy, sense customer satisfaction, see how strategy is being delivered, and most importantly, feel the pulse of the company.

Insubordination vs. Treason

On a number of occasions, I have had the opportunity of working with CEOs who had problems with managers that required special attention. The problem usually boiled down to a situation where a manager or executive had objected to a particular decision that had been made by the CEO. The

53

problem occurs because the dissenting manager saw the decision as being bad for the company. Or s/he saw it as being inconsistent with the defined strategy. In other situations, the dissenting manager or executive made the objection as a way to challenge the authority of the CEO.

In either case, what do you do? Do you allow insubordination? My answer is yes. Because it is only through No Blame and rebellious, honest dissent can you encourage managers to offer objection to ideas that haven't been cleanly or clearly defined. As a CEO you have to have confidence in your managers that they are offering objections because they care about the company. So you have to allow for the insubordination that might occur when a manager steps up and objects to a decision that has been made. At some point, the objection has been discussed, data re-examined and a new decision is made or the old one stands, in either case, the insubordination had better become support or the issue of treason arises.

As for treason, this is a more difficult situation. If in the situation noted above, the dissenting manager fails to get on board after additional consideration is given to the objection, then it is possible that treason needs to be considered. I call it treason because when a CEO is involved with the War on Waste (and it is an ongoing initiative) and a direct order is refused after significant discussion, then treason has occurred. Treason is a capital offense. In the political milieu, it means death. In the War on Waste, it means termination.

Let me give you a good example of how this might occur. In one company, the CEO had called a staff meeting. All of his executives and key managers were in attendance, including his son, who was one of the managers. His son was the heir apparent and was a bit on the feisty side. He was aggressive, smart and impatient. He did not like anyone to challenge him. His father had asked me to help him control his harangues at meetings and to teach him about business manners. I liked the young man because I could see a lot of his father in him. But he could be a jerk at times. In this particular meeting, the son had made a proposal. He had not thoroughly analyzed the consequences of his recommendation and began to get angry when various other managers started to object to key parts of his proposal. You could see his glare. It was nasty.

One manager, who I really liked, was particularly rough on the young heir. He thought that the idea was a bad one and didn't mince any words about it. The young heir was beginning to lose it and accused the dissenting manager of treason. The dissenting manager was not willing to back down because he knew he was right and pointed out to him that he didn't care what his opinion was anyway because he couldn't do anything about that because deciding treason was his father's responsibility.

At that point, the father broke in and told everyone to cool down. As the CEO, he told everyone that the discussion had been good. He had heard enough and had decided to table the discussion and created a committee of three (the son, the dissenting manager and me) to resolve the issues and come up with a recommendation at the next meeting to either: fix the issues, table the idea forever, or collect more data.

I have to admit that was one of the greatest challenges that I have ever had as a consultant. The heir apparent was going to be there, the dissenting manager was a valuable employee and the issue that the heir apparent had raised was worthy of further analysis. We did that, the young heir had a chance to spend more time with this manager and appreciate his value and the manager had a chance to make a valuable contribution to the company.

Trust me, it is never easy to distinguish between "insubordination" and "treason." But recognize that there is a difference and give the dissenting employee the benefit of the doubt.

American Management Paradox

A paradox, as defined by Webster's, is a statement that seems contradictory, unbelievable, or absurd, but that may also be true in fact. What I am calling the American Management Paradox arose from an observation of a friend, who was always amused by Americans (he was from Canada). He had figured out that America's strength, as a country, was a paradox. According to him, Americans have a strong sense of individualism but they possess a fierce competitive drive to compete—and yet, when Americans put people in corporations, we take away the employee's sense of individualism. We make the individual conform. My friend's observation was that if you could define an organization that managed the individualism but did so by placing the individual in a work environment that encouraged competition between work teams, a strong organization would evolve.

He felt that a good management system would benefit by using this paradox to its advantage by restoring to the employee his or her individualism. Naturally that is a challenge.

And that is what we do in the War on Waste. We start by allowing employees to express their individualism when they rise in the classroom to identify a waste. And we protect them with No Blame. A top-down, highly structured organization is going to try to get conformity in its management of employees. They are going to be managed and the spirit of individual

56

War on Waste Innovation

achievement is going to be crushed. So in the War on Waste, we create a pathway for ideas that challenge the status quo. We want ideas. And an environment that supports ideas and renegade sources of these ideas is a bit different.

This company is fun for the employees and profitable for the owners. As ornery and independent as many of these people are, this new organization is fragile in that a malevolent manager can do significant damage in resisting the movement to the new culture. We call these people "Black Knights" (see later). They get their name from the character in the Monte Python movie, "In Search of the Holy Grail". The Black Knight failed to admit his problems and was in total denial that he had a problem (he was missing his arms and legs). These creatures can destroy a War on Waste program. Our job as facilitators has always been to convert them or crush them when they fail to convert. We do this with the CEOs backing. If the CEO has hired us to do a War on Waste, then getting rid of obstacles to its success is very important.

One of the ways that we get the individualists to participate in the improvement of the business is to make participation a game. We introduce the concept of World Records (See "World Record Reports" – page 76) as a way to get people thinking of competition. Break a world record and get recognized. The world record is explained later but it is very simply a way to put different teams up against each other and measuring their performance against the best they have ever done and in many cases, the best that any team has done. And boy did the teams of individualists love the competition. They had to work within their teams to compete. It was a "Three Musketeers" mindset: "All for one and one for all."

But this works, trust me. If a CEO wants to know how to get the game started, read the segment on World Record

Reports. [Or if you want to read a story about it, read "The Tribal Knowledge Paradox – Using the War on Waste to Align Strategy with Process" by this author[8].]

The paradox presents management in the United States with a big challenge. It boils down to saying that management has to avoid confusing shareholders, employees and customers by saying one thing and doing another. This is the basis of the paradox that serves as the central thesis of the "Tribal Knowledge Paradox."

CEO's 6 Best Practices Guidelines

Every CEO has many things to do. The following 6 things define the core part of the guidelines for every CEOs job from our perspective. They are:

1. Manage Strategy;

2. Improve Tribal Knowledge;

3. Oversee key hires;

4. Develop and manage the company culture;

5. Manage change;

6. Manage innovation;

Let me try to explain each point.

Manage Strategy – I think this is obvious. But it always isn't so obvious how it might affect a CEO. For instance, when I sell the WOW program to a company, I try to make the sales pitch to the CEO on the presumption that WOW will help to re-align strategy with process when it is implemented. So when a company elects to take on a WOW program, it needs to get

---

War on Waste Innovation

CEO approval because of the effect on strategy. In fact, if you look at unsuccessful Lean Manufacturing or 6 Sigma programs they fail when the CEO is not involved.

It turns out they also fail when they focus the action on the Black Belt trainers and not those doing the projects. But that is part of another discussion on why initiatives like WOW can fail.

The Board of Directors gives the CEO the responsibility of managing strategy. This is an unwritten rule of business. I often go into companies and find that the COO or the CFO talk as if they are implementing strategy in their department. I usually point out to them that I was under the impression that the CEO alone was responsible for strategy and they are usually taken aback. So I go to the CEO and get straight on this. In most cases, the issue isn't lack of clarity of job responsibility, it is lack of clarity of what strategy is. On further analysis, the various other C-Level Executives were just confusing tactics with strategy.

Improve Corporate Tribal Knowledge – Five of the guidelines that I've noted above are generally accepted aspects of a CEO's job. But this particular issue is probably the most critical in managing Innovation, new products and know-how. But it probably is not on anyone's radar. Innovation, new products and know-how are the lifeblood of any organization. They are the drivers of internal growth. And, they need to be managed.

But there is a subtle thing here that makes this responsibility of a CEO so important. When we delivered the first War on Waste programs, we recognized the value of paying attention to Tribal Knowledge. But we failed to recognize that the key here was not just to add energy in the form of an initiative type program. We also needed to use the initial energy infusion from the War on Waste or a comparable program to set in motion a continuous flow of energy into the company. This comes from new ideas and innovations. And that is how we came up with the design for the Tribal Knowledge Paradigm.

The key was recognizing that even though the CEO was the key support point, every manager had to be involved. Improving Tribal Knowledge or know-how needed to be a touchstone of management not just a major event that infused energy in a one-time event. This is accomplished with a paradigm that "encourages improvements in Tribal Knowledge" as a fundamental tenet for managers.

This is a basic responsibility of managers. Once the initial energy kick is provided by the initiative, the goal of this paradigm is to maintain that energy level with primary support from the management staff. Ideas are to be encouraged and supported. Process improvement ideas should be the norm. Ideas for new product innovations are to be sought and supported. In other words, the Tribal Knowledge Paradigm creates a Culture of Innovation.

Oversee key hires – This goes without saying. The CEO must be involved in the hiring of any C-Level Executive but s/he must be involved in all key hires. It is important that the CEO impart his stamp of approval on all these recruits for a number of reasons.

One, if he doesn't, others may perceive a lack of commitment to a particular new manager and company personnel are quick to pick up on this. Another reason is the CEO has to sense the type of character that he wants in new key hires. A bad apple is certainly not wanted and the CEO can use his keen senses to ferret them out.

War on Waste Innovation

Develop and Manage the Company Culture – Very little is said about this but it goes without saying that the CEO defines and supports the company culture. Whether it is his culture, a previous CEO's or the company founder's, it is the CEO's responsibility to clearly state and support it.

I know that Hewlett Packard's culture was clearly stated by its founders. It was the "HP Way" which was a unique blend of profits and people that had existed for over 50 years. All employees at the company bought into it and lived it. But when Carly Fiorina tried to mess with it, she ran into huge resistance from the troops. Although managing the culture was her responsibility, the culture was so entrenched that she encountered huge resistance when she tried to change it.

She wanted to reorganize business structures that would have made HP more efficient and more competitive. But the employees resisted. After she was ousted, Mark Hurd came in and ended up doing much of what Fiorina had tried to do but he did so in the framework of the HP Way and he succeeded. He had to lay-off a large number of people to get back into the game. And that was not the HP Way. But it was necessary to complete the realignment of resources necessary for success in the current business climate.

It is interesting that over the 25 plus years that I have delivered the War on Waste, I have seen major changes in company cultures. These occurred as the CEOs responded to the positive contributions of employees. It is fun to see how management that supports employee ideas during the War on Waste is not only a fun business to manage, but a profitable one. So we have coined a term to describe the resulting culture. We call it the "Quantum Leap Company" because of the dramatic change of the culture that results from WOW

61

programs. (See page 127) It is a major jump or a quantum leap of change in the business organization and performance.

Manage Change – This is a more subtle part of the job. One could say that managing change is part of managing the culture but change in itself is strategic in its effect on a company. If a change has no affect on profits or revenue, it is not strategic but if it does, it is.

So when I come into a company and implement the War on Waste, I am affecting revenue and profits big time and so the management of this process is a CEO responsibility from its impact on strategy. But change in itself is not strategic. It can be when it helps to align strategy with process. So I make a point of telling CEOs that this is part of their job so that they can be alerted to actions that lead to change that lead to improvements in profits and revenues. That can sneak up on a CEO if s/he is not attentive to change as a specific job responsibility.

So when we tried a couple of early WOW projects without CEO involvement, we got push back from the CEO in a big way. So my involvement in these situations was to get in front of the CEO and explain what the program was about. There were usually some concessions. The CEOs didn't like them but they agreed to them because they made the company more profitable.

It turns out that these CEOs understood their job intuitively. Because it was not spelled out as the CEOs job responsibility, other executives felt free to initiate their own "change programs" without CEO approval. By stating this as a job responsibility of the CEO, everyone knows it and acts accordingly.

War on Waste Innovation

Manage Innovation – It turns out that the War on Waste is all about innovation. Most of the innovation is what we call "incremental innovation" in the framework of innovation that was defined by Peter Drucker.

He defined 4 types of innovation: incremental, disruptive, organizational and new business. You can think of most of the ideas that we get in the War on Waste as incremental ideas. They are $100,000 of waste that can be fixed for an investment of less than $2,000. They are the low hanging fruit that we hear about. Or they are the nuggets of gold that we kick around the business and fail to pick up.

For example, it is the remote lock on a car. It was not a big deal because it evolved from technology like the garage door opener. It was just technology applied in a unique way. Maybe it was patented but it was not a big deal. It was just a cool deal.

Or maybe another example is the faster microprocessor in the semiconductor industry. The Intel 8085 was incremental innovation after the major disruption of the market created by the phenomenal success of the Intel 8080. The 8085 added some bells and whistles but the bulk of the innovation occurred with the Intel 8080. That was truly a disruptive innovation.

However, there are very interesting low hanging fruit that can turn into the disruptive innovation that creates the quantum leap for a company. In the auto world the mini-van was a disruptive innovation because it radically changed the family automobile market. The IBM PC was a disruptive and radical change in the computer field. It was not the first PC. It was the first one that provided a practical and useful integration of software and hardware that made it work. It made the distributed computer network possible. More importantly, it

Leonard Bertain, Ph.D.

gave individuals a way to use technology to advance themselves. And that is a big deal.

In WOW programs, we have had low cost innovations allow a radical cost reduction in the processing of DNA segments used in research in the genetics-engineering field. This particular development allowed the company to secure major contracts and disrupt the competition for these important research chemicals. This was an exciting blend of treachery and cunning to make it work. This is a good story.

The CEO of the business needed to be kept out of the loop until the product prototype was completed. Once that was done, the process of creating the completed full-production products was an easy path. But to get there, a lot of effort was required behind the scenes. The fun part was that it worked.

In organizational innovation, the Saturn organizational structure was dramatically different from the traditional GM business. In the computer field, iTunes was initially a shift in the traditional organization of Apple because it forced Apple to respond to the unique requirements of managing a media distribution business. Its average price per sale went from $1,000 to $1. It was a totally new market for Apple.

We have seen this in WOW programs in two distinct ways: one, when new products are created and another with old products are upgraded with new technology (new applications of the old technology). In both cases, a new management structure is required to reach new customers and new distribution channels.

And finally, a new venture innovation might be iTunes as it became a full contributor to the profits of Apple as a separate organization. Or it might also be IBM's PC Division. It was a radical new business for IBMers who were known in the

War on Waste Innovation

industry as the "Suits". There was never an IBM organization that allowed employees to come to work in anything but coat and tie. It was not only disruptive; it was a radical change within IBM.

So when I work with CEOs, they need to learn what these 4 types of innovations are so that when I am no longer there, they will be able to see these innovations as they are unfolding in the initial stages of ideation. If they pay attention, they can move an incremental innovation idea to a very profitable disruptive innovation.

This is a learned skill and evolves over time. We encourage CEOs to get involved with the idea process. After the War on Waste, ideas start to flow and they need to be managed in what we call the Tribal Knowledge Council. It is described in the next section (See page 93). It is one of the tools of the War on Waste. It is where ideas are tracked through the process.

Leonard Bertain, Ph.D.

War on Waste Tools

We have used a number of tools to help identify and analyze a waste. These tools have evolved from others of greater insight as well as from our own unique look at the problems of identifying, quantifying and getting rid of wastes. How we look at the root cause of the waste and the way that we measure our accomplishments is often unique.

War on Waste Innovation

Act – Learn – Improve -Act

(Actio-Eruditio-Confectio). This is our motto. As we deliver the War on Waste, we lead employees through a process that requires them to analyze the size of the waste or the effect of the waste on the company in terms of lost profits or sales. Trying to do this is not easy. But it happens because the employees have a goal of finding an answer to a question that they know is costing the company money. And they really get into it. They love the action created by the War on Waste.

As the process unfolds, teaching tools and techniques are introduced when they are needed to help frame a problem in a different light or use a new tool to stretch their thinking (book learnin'), the War on Waste begins with classroom analysis and activity. We push our clients' employees to begin implementing the smallest changes right away. So one might say that our model is: Act-learn-improve-act.

This is not an insignificant difference; the other strategies for major organizational change begin with education and training. They are apparently based on the model: learn-act. The problem with this model is that is not how most humans really operate. Most people act and learn from their experience. So, when an organization really wants to change the patterns of work, it is very ineffective to teach employees tools and methods, and then expect them to find ways to use them. It is much more sensible to move them to work on changing work processes, and provide them with the tools they need, when they need them.

The War on Waste begins with No Blame. The No Blame raises the banner of protection for ideas and the actions that those ideas demand. The War on Waste is all about improving a business using a systematic approach to analyzing inefficiencies in business processes. It doesn't take much

67

thought to understand what this is about. It simply means that when an action is taken, no one is going to be blamed in the War on Waste system for doing something. You may be asked to explain a particular action when the results aren't as expected but you will never be blamed. You are expected to learn from your action. Make any appropriate improvements and act again.

In our work with companies doing War on Waste projects, we can quickly move employees to action. But you can trust me that they won't move on anything without our laying down protection to them with No Blame. Employees are reluctant to make any suggestions without the protection of No Blame and the support of the CEO. In this system, we want employees to come up with ideas and do what it takes to make them happen. So as an action is taking place we want employees to: act-learn-improve. The War on Waste is all about action. In other words, act (do something that will eliminate a waste that has been identified), learn (learn from what you have done), and improve (correct the problems of your earlier actions and act again).

To many, this might seem trivial. It might even seem very obvious but it isn't from our experiences. Owners of businesses get very frustrated over this because their employees are not entirely comfortable taking action after years of being restrained from inputting ideas into their companies. So we get really excited when we see employees following our motto. It means that they are comfortable putting an idea into play. They are accepting of the concept that things may not always go as expected and they know that the owner will not berate them for a failed or less than successful effort. This is big time stuff. It is exciting to watch. When an employee makes the jump to buy into "act-learn-improve" it is an act of commitment to a management concept.

War on Waste Innovation

And with that commitment comes more new ideas. We call this management approach, the Tribal Knowledge Paradigm.

Bibeault 120/20 Rule of Profits

There is a corollary to the 80/20 Rule that really gives us greater insight into the happenings in business. A consulting friend showed me this rule. We all know it: 120% of a company's profits come from 20% of the customers, 20% of the salesmen, or 20% of the products or services. I call it the Bibeault 120/20 Rule of Profits, in honor of my consultant friend who pointed it out to me.[9] The reason that this rule is so important in developing an effective customer-driven strategy is that it will truly allow us to focus our attention on those customers who deliver the most profit to the company. It may also provide substantial information to focus us while we try to understand why these customers are more profitable.

Consider this example with one client. This particular customer had about 100 customers. 40 of these customers accounted for about 90% of his business. The lowest 40 customers accounted for less than 5% of his business. We analyzed his accounts and found that about 40% of his bidding activity was consumed by the bottom 5%. In a sales department, it is difficult to measure profitability. Don't get hung up here. Take the simple approach.

So we did. We established that each phone call to a customer or visit to a customer was given a point. Each bid was given 50 points. These then translated into points of overhead. We then used these points to measure how much

---

[9] Don Bibeault is a venture capital investor now. In his former life, he was management consultant who specialized in turning around distressed companies.

Leonard Bertain, Ph.D.

activity was required by each customer for each dollar of bidding and then measured how many dollars were won. So when the salesmen had to decide where they were going to spend their time, they basically went for the customers that had the fewest points per dollar of resulting bids won. A simple formula but it worked.

The interesting corollary to this rule is that the only way for this rule to exist it exists is if some of the customers, salesmen, products or services are unprofitable.

Unlike the 80/20 rule, which only deals with positive numbers, the 120/20 rule allows for negative numbers--losses." (see following figure).

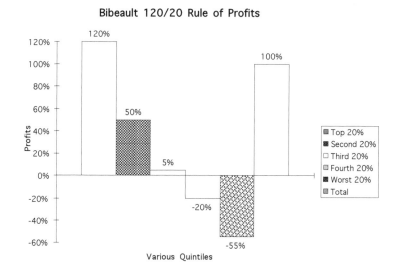

In the case of unprofitable customers, salesmen, products or services, additional analysis needs to be determined whether or not they are worth keeping. Or put another way, this rule helps you determine whether all customers really should be kept.

I remember giving a talk where one CEO in the audience had a grin on his face after I mentioned the "120/20 rule of profits." His mind was working and I wouldn't have noticed him if he hadn't made a big deal out of opening his briefcase to pull out a notebook. He started writing furiously; clearly his mind was working. Afterwards, he came up, thanked me for my great insight, and he left hurriedly. The next day, he called me to tell me what he had done.

He owned a business and he had five salesmen. One of the five salesmen generated 60% of his revenue and about 150% of the profits. One of the other salesmen took up all his time, always complained about the products that they didn't have, the orders that he was going to lose, and so on. The CEO went back to the office, called the non-productive salesman into his office, and fired him immediately. He realized while I was talking that it wasn't that the guy was bad, he just kept the CEO from being able to provide support to the other salesman. In fact, what he did changed the sales organization to help the successful salesman make more proposals and had the other three 3 salesmen support him. And it was a good deal for everyone, because everyone made more money. I don't know if that was the right move but he calls me regularly to thank me and still takes me out to lunch at least once a quarter to pick my brain for more ideas.

As a corollary to the 120/20 Rule, Don Bibeault also has another axiom: "Feed the winners, starve the losers." His position here is that if you have a winning product or salesman, do everything to make them as successful as you can. However, when you have a loser, don't terminate them or end their product development effort immediately, just cut back on the financial support to see what happens. Some times, the failure is timing in a particular market or maybe not enough time available to complete the project for whatever reason. But if you have a salesman or a new product that is failing, don't kill them, just reduce the resources available because there are a lot of successes that failed in their initial efforts and by dribbling funds to the team involved, you never know. But once you have played that card to its limit, you cut your losses, but not without first trying.

This line of thinking fits well with our work with the 5/67 Rule. This is 5% of the effort gets 67% of the results. When a CEO is doling out money for new products, he should try doing a product with 5% of the features (gets you to the market quickly) and see what happens. It's amazing how much information is extracted from the market this way.

On this subject, one of my associates refers to his mentor from graduate school who was a former CEO at Warner Lambert. This CEO used to say that it was counter-intuitive, but he knew that he was doing a good job when 50% of his projects were successful. His reason for saying this is a corollary to the 5/67 Rule. You never know all that you think you know when you release a product and going with a few features and releasing the product quickly with good customer feedback, you could get more useful information to guide your decision to spend more money on a product that may be a loser. His conclusion was to "feed the winners (with more money) and starve the losers (with less money). Good advice? I think so.

Cycle time

Cycle time is defined as the time it takes a particular value-added product or service to be completed once it starts through the value-added process. Lead-time is the time from the

War on Waste Innovation

receipt of an order or service until it is delivered and paid for. We emphasize "and paid for" because that is when the lead-time stops, not when you ship it. The following examples illustrate what we mean by cycle time. (See also "Lead time" below)

Examples:

Machine shop -The time it takes to make and prepare to ship a part. This includes the full cycle of operations to complete the part: machining, deburring, and cleaning. In a machine shop the cycle time may be a couple of days, while the lead-time may be several weeks. Ideally, the goal of a good machine shop is to make the cycle time as close to the lead-time as possible. If you do that, your customer will not have to keep large inventories of parts.

Medical Facility - The time it takes to process a patient through a surgical procedure. This would include such functions as: preparing the patient with a sedative, moving the patient to prep room, the doctor cleaning up for surgery, the preparation of the surgical facility, the operation, the closing-up procedure, the waking of the patient from anesthesia, and moving the patient back to a room. The lead-time would be from the patient entering the hospital until s/he leaves and the insurance company pays the bill.

Dry Cleaners - The actual process of cleaning the suit in solvent, drying it in a dryer, pressing, hanging, and bagging it for storage.

Lead-time

The time it takes for your business to deliver a product/service from the time it is ordered until cash is received for performing the value. You notice that lead time is linked to when the product is paid for because if you ship parts late, ship the wrong parts, ship poor quality parts, etc. the customer is not going to pay until the transaction is complete. And that happens when the customer is satisfied with the product or service. If either is badly delivered, then payment will be delayed. And that will extend the lead-time and make it longer.

A number of business friends have questioned the logic of this definition. The standard lead-time is defined as the time from when an order is received for the product or service until the product or service is shipped or delivered. I just think that it allows for sloppy measurement and doesn't hold the back end part of the transaction, those who ship the product, accountable.

Examples:

Machine shop - The time it takes for the product to move through the machine shop from the receipt of purchase order until the client pays for the part or parts.

Medical facility - The time it takes from planning for the surgery until it is completed, the patient leaves the hospital, and the insurance company pays the last installment (reluctantly after 30 phone calls).

Dry cleaners - The time from when the customer drops the clothes off until they are picked up and paid for.

New Product Lead Time – Perhaps the greatest application of the lead-time concept is in tracking the lead-time for a new product. My reason for saying this is an experience that I had with an executive from one of the auto companies. When I asked the CFO, if he only had one number to measure a company's success, what would that be. He said profit of course. But I told him that I thought it was Product Lead Time because it tells you how innovation is

War on Waste Innovation

working and how engineering is working with pilot production with full production and, finally, with sales.

Remember that lead-time is the time from the inception of the idea for a new car until it was shipped to the sales floor and sold. That is usually a long time. In this company, a well-known product had taken 66 months to get thru their process to market while the Japanese were only taking 32 months at the time. Both the CFO and the CEO acknowledged the importance and in a major TV ad, this CEO was bragging to America that a new product had taken only 36 months to get to market. And he was proud of that. Today, Toyota can get a new car to market in less than 18 months.

Data Gathering Rules

When gathering information during a War on Waste project, the No Blame principle and the Scientific Method require that all participants be aware that the pursuit of honest and accurate information is one of the most important parts of the process. It is usually very easy to come up with solutions. But the process of proving that there is a problem is sometimes quite difficult. So we encourage teams during the War on Waste to follow the following principles of the Scientific Method:

Demand evidence – In the War on Waste, employees are asked to prove to the CEO that there is a problem. To do so, they must collect data that is both honest and accurate. It must be collected but sometimes, Black Knights get in the way. And that's when the CEO must get involved. If anyone gets in the way of the data collection process, they must be made aware immediately that they are standing in treasonous shoes. We see this as probably the most significant problem in the War on Waste. There are people who allege that they are guarding precious information. And when someone below them in the organization demands to look at the information that is being "protected" these Black Knights begin their evil deeds. Once the CEO gets involved, the problem will get resolved.

Be willing to speculate – One of the greatest projects that I worked on with a client was one in which three very junior employees had begun to investigate the value-added contribution of a particular process. They were trying to collect information but a Black Knight was getting in the way. They didn't tell me this until two days before their presentation was due. I went to the CEO and told him of the problem, he got involved and got the information that they needed. They then proceeded to analyze the data. In the mean time, the President told me what he expected their findings to be. I told the team that I had written down what the CEO expected their findings to be. They analyzed the data in about 2 hours, and low and behold, the CEO was right. I told them that since the CEO was a scientist, he speculated on the outcome of every experiment. That is what made him such a good scientist. Just like this CEO, we encourage our War on Waste teams to speculate on the outcomes of their data collection process. It doesn't hurt and it makes for good War on Waste training and good science.

Inquire about incongruities - I am amazed at how obvious some problems are to hourly employees but not to managers. They see incongruities for what they really are: lack of clarity on the part of management. The issues are usually incongruities that employees see in what management says it wants to do versus what it does. For instance, one company told the company employees and its customers that it was a "just in time" supplier. But the employees knew that to be a JIT supplier the company needed to produce parts in smaller batches. But did the company do anything to reduce the sizes of batches? No. And the employees knew that was stupid. A true scientific investigation encourages employees to note these problems and check them out. These incongruities are usually big wastes.

Question with innocence and ignorance – The War on Waste begins with an acknowledgement of No Blame as the ruling philosophy. In many cases, the questions that employees ask are innocent explorations of how things work in the company. Managers need to become leaders in helping their charges to understand how things work, or should work. If employees are allowed to pursue the search for "the truth", then great things are possible. To do this, companies must allow employees this pursuit of information with an inquisitiveness that is free from fear. We use the term "innocence" to describe this search because it in many cases the War on Waste provides these workers with a forum on which to pursue the unknowns of how a business "really" works. And to many, the leaders of the company must help make this search an exciting and rewarding experience.

Encourage questions - There are no stupid questions. So listen to them all. As a scientist, I always felt that the greatest progress was made once people knew what question to ask. And we find that is really true in the War on Waste. It is from questions, that we seek answers. But the questions come first.

Challenge conventional wisdom – My mother used to begin her doctrinaire positions with "They say…" Of course, I never did find out who "they" were. But now I think of "them" as conventional wisdom. And others may call them "sacred cows." Whatever, "sacred cows make good burgers."

Seek explanations for new and puzzling things – Part of the Scientific Paradigm is trying to explain what is going on. We want to encourage employees to try to understand things that don't make sense. In one company, an employee couldn't understand why the assembly process of a particular product took one person 1 1/2 minutes to put together, but a team of 3 was taking almost 2 minutes. It didn't make sense. So he asked a manager and they researched the "puzzle" and found that they really only needed one person to do that particular assembly and 3 people were getting in each other's way. So they were able to set up 3 separate assembly operations when the team got around to that particular assembly again. And they got 3 times the production. The net result was an overall reduction in the direct labor component of costs of about 1%.

Eighty-Twenty (80/20) Rule

This is probably the most important tool in business. We know from this rule that: 80% of your problems come from 20% of your customers; 80% of your revenue comes from 20% of your customers, and so forth. As you look at the data, you hope that the same 20% of the customers that create all your problems are not the same ones that generate all your revenue.

When I first started doing this consulting over 25 years ago, consulting friends told me that the 80/20 Rule was a sacred tool of the consultant. Actually, what he meant was, the 80/20 rule helped guide the solutions of more problems in business than any other, and in the hands of a consultant, it is was a sacred tool for making money. It has always been there for me to steady a project. As far as I am concerned, however, it is and always was there to help guide my thinking. It is not just reserved for the exclusive use of consultants. It is a tool for everyone. As a facilitator, whenever I get stuck on a problem, I think about how the 80/20 Rule might help.

I have some good examples but let me tell a story of how I first learned about the 80/20 Rule. My father owned a laundry business. When I was in high school and college, I used to do

War on Waste Innovation

the maintenance for him, and I often needed to spend money to fix things. Whenever I went to my father to ask for $100, like for a tool, he would give me $20 and see what I could do. If I needed $500, he gave me $100. Being somewhat analytical, I put two and two together and figured that every time I asked for any amount of money, my Dad always gave me 20% of the requested amount. And it always turned out that he never got more than about 80% of the desired result. I never really got to fix things right. I was always putting band-aids on problems.

Years later, I asked him if he knew that he was invoking the 80/20 rule. He didn't, and he asked, "What's that?" I told him, and boy did he laugh. He laughed and then said, "you didn't know that I such great intuitive understanding of business did you?" he said. Then I had to laugh.

Let me give you some other examples.

On my first consulting job assignment as an independent, I was working with four shop workers in a manufacturing plant. The President of the company gave us an assignment. He told us to figure out something that would make him a lot of money. In other words, identify a problem and propose a solution. So we began to figure out what problem we were going to solve.

We began by asking what products accounted for significant revenues. After asking that question, one of the workers immediately had an idea. He knew that there was one model of product that accounted for over 25% of sales and that it had a 20-week backlog. The backlog accounted for 80% of the company's total backlog. In this case, we had found 20% of the business (actually 25%) that accounted for 80% of the backlog that was 6 weeks or more. After we completed the development of a cell to deal with this product line, we reduced the backlog to 2 weeks in a very short time, and the product

79

Leonard Bertain, Ph.D.

ended up generating about 40% of the business and over 60% of the company profits.

In summary, this story illustrates how we were able to identify an opportunity using the 80/20 rule and with good data to direct our confidence that the problem was worth doing. We then came up with a great solution that paid great dividends to the company.

Another application of the 80/20 Rule occurs quite often when employees get into the War on Waste. I ask them to identify problems, but I don't give them unlimited budgets to solve the problem. We ask employees to find problems that amount to $100,000 of annual waste. When we impose a spending limit to spending of less than $2,000, we force employees to think creatively. By putting that restriction on employees as they work through the War on Waste, you force them to understand the value of scaling the problem down to deal with only 20% of the problem and see how much of the benefit can be achieved. For example, a team finds that the waste of set-ups accounts for $1.5 Million in lost revenue. A great solution might be adding a pallet changer to speed up the time for set-ups for a cost of $25,000. I go back to the employees and say, I can't give you $25,000 but I can give you $5,000. In other words, I am going to give you 20% of the total cost that you need. Now see what you can get for me with that. In most cases, the 80% benefit is achieved: 80% of the benefit is achieved by spending 20% of the expected cost. And $1.2 Million in benefits (80%) might be achieved with a manual pallet changing system that costs $4,000.

One of the interesting things that happen during the War on Waste is that the 80/20 rule guides project teams to pick low hanging fruit. In other words, spend only as much as you need to make a dent in the waste. Sometimes the waste is so big that

War on Waste Innovation

it is like eating the elephant. How do you do that? A bite at a time! Our War on Waste projects usually amount to small bites out of the total company waste. And when we target only $100,000 of annual waste that can be fixed for a cost of less than $2,000, we are getting employees to focus on those items that have the biggest bang for the buck.

So when a company tries to do automation projects after the War on Waste, it is hard to justify the automation investment based on minor inefficiency improvements. The automation project is usually a capital investment. It means spending money to change the way a company does business and who its customers might become. The automation project that goes in after the War on Waste is usually strategic in nature. In these capital expenditures, we try to find investments that improve revenue per production employee. This keeps the focus on productivity. But it also drives decisions to look at both the efficiency of the process and the hourly rate per employee needed to maintain the new equipment.

I mention this because years ago when I first started consulting I did work in CIM (Computer Integrated Manufacturing) Systems. The way that we got the early stage funding was to show the dramatic improvement in business processes that resulted from the automation. In fact, the automation was actually a multiple stage process. We called the first phase "Phase 0" and it was a different version of the War on Waste. It targeted process inefficiencies. We then argued to our clients that these quick fixes were really good because they generated cash quickly. The cash was then used to pay for the subsequent automation phases that consisted of: preliminary technical specification, prototype development, implementation testing (test whether the prototype worked),

81

Leonard Bertain, Ph.D.

full project specification, implementation, testing and measurements determining the project's success.

When we were all done with our CIM projects, they resembled our work with the War on Waste. We targeted a waste: we used the 80/20 rules to guide us in partitioning the waste down to a small problem that could be implemented with the small $2,000 allowance. Once the waste was eliminated and the measurements told us so, we then looked at automation opportunities.

We have used the 80/20 rule to help us in banks (80% of the loan cycle time was consumed by 20% of the loan steps); in distribution companies (80% of the total items picked in a warehouse come from 20% of the items – this is a helpful concept in laying out the design of a warehouse); Materials management (MRP systems are based almost entirely upon the 80/20 rule – pay attention to the 20% of the items that account for 80% of your inventory value). The 80/20 Rule applies everywhere and it is good to know what it means.

5/67 Rule

The 5/67 Rule is a subset of the 20/80 Rule or 80/20 Rule. We discovered it during the War on Waste. We were always in a hurry to get projects completed and we didn't have time to look at 20% of the problem demanded by the 20/80 Rule. But we did have time to look at 5% of the problem. And when we did that we kept seeing that we were getting about 60 to 70% of the targeted benefit. We called it the 5/67 Rule without really knowing much about it. It just seemed to work but it didn't make sense until we stepped back and looked at what was happening.

It turns out that what we were seeing was effectively the 20/80 Rule operating on the 20/80 Rule. If you take 20% of

War on Waste Innovation

20%, you get 4%. And if you take 80% of 80%, you get 64%. And the 4% and the 64% were close enough to 5% and 67% and that is how we got there.

We think that 5/67 thinking is the way that you should run a business. For instance, when you develop a new product, deliver 5% of the features and you will get 67% of the benefit and then you can add other features over time. The rationale here is that 5% of the features gets you to market quickly. The 5% of the features can serve as the foundation for building an aggressive product expansion plan. It gives you a jump on the competition and you have your progressive plan of features available to quickly introduce new versions of the product.

My theory on new products is that you want to get the product off the shelf quickly and immediately begin generating profits. The problem with most developments of new products is that the engineer is never satisfied until s/he has delivered the 100% solution. That is folly and is very expensive. Get the product to the market, use the profits to pay for expansion and improvements and be recognized as an intelligent source of great innovation.

Managers and executives that I have worked with need about 2 seconds to understand why there is a problem letting engineers work to get the "100% Solution." My point is that it will take forever and cost a fortune. So I advise CEOs to get the product out the door and see if anyone actually likes it or wants it. Once on the market, new features can be added. Of course, you need to anticipate as many of those future features as you can to minimize the costs of upgrades, but if you start generating revenue you can start adding staff to move to a more complete offering. There are many others more knowledgeable about how to do this but trust me, if you adopt a "5/67 Design Mentality," you will be very successful and profitable.

In fact, I have a theory based upon this principle. It is the Bertain Theory of why electronic tradeshows exist. I talk about it later but it boils to this. If you didn't have a trade show to give an engineer a target for product completion, it would never get done. I have theories about this that I go into later (see Page 163). And all of this is based upon the 5/67 Rule. Just get it to market and do it quickly.

Measurement

We think that our approach to performance improvement is unique in how we teach our clients to measure performance. Our philosophy about measurement is very simple but has profound implications. We believe that measurement must be a tool for each member of the organization, a tool that guides him/her to continually improve performance.

Before you begin to nod that this is only common sense, this is not what we see in the great percentage of organizations and how they use measurements. Measurement in these companies is a tool for managers, a flag that alerts them to problems or deviations from the norm; typically, the measures are well after the fact. They are too late to guide performance.

Our approach to measurement is to develop measures that let employees know how the work is proceeding, what needs to be done, and what can be expected. We do not measure individuals; we measure the work. When we define work, it is:

➡ **Plan** (Planning the work)

➡ **Control** (Controlling the work)

    o **Measure**

War on Waste Innovation

o **Adjust**

➡ **Do** (Doing the Work)

The usual question that we ask workers in the War on Waste is who does the planning. Of course, they aren't involved in the planning of the work, the managers are. But who gets to do the work? Of course, it is the workers. So as we get into the War on Waste, we begin to get everyone to understand what we mean by "work."

So when we talk about control, we mean that we measure the work and then adjust the results if the measurement isn't what we expect it to be. Measurement is a way to keep score of how well work (value-added or essential support activity) is being done. And the work is done under the banner of "No Blame" so that we can get "honest data." We want honest data so that we can believe it. We want employees to feel comfortable that they can report data as it is and make the numbers believable.

Our philosophy is that if you can believe the measurement, it can be improved. If it can't, question the need for the activity. Measurement is intended to improve the output of the organization, not the control of the manager. Measurement is thus a tool for the workers, not the managers. This doesn't mean that managers can't know what the measures are; it's just not their primary job to use the measurements to adjust performance. In the traditional measurement, the measures are well after the fact. They are too late to guide performance.

(See additional information on measurement in the segments on "Yes/No Charts" and "World Record Reports")

85

Leonard Bertain, Ph.D.

Yes/No Charts

Perhaps one of the most powerful tools that I have developed is the "Yes/No Chart." I say that it is powerful, not because I am enamored of the invention, but because I am ecstatic by the results of this very simple tool.

What is a "Yes/No" chart? Very simply, it is a chart that is set up to measure a result. It answers a simple question, a question whose answer is yes or no. In this measurement, "maybe" is not an acceptable answer. In fact, the chart has only two allowable marks, either "yes" or "no." There is no third category: "perhaps", "maybe", "sometime", etc. The answer is given on a "No Blame" basis; we want to know what is truly happening.

The way that this idea developed has a funny history. At the pilot company, we had talked about No Blame and someone in the class raised the issue of the truck leaving late every day. The minute that was mentioned a hush went over the room. I knew something was going on. So I asked the obvious question, why is it a problem when the truck leaves late? No one responded. So I was trying to figure out a way to get to the end of this story. So I went out to the shipping area and put up the first Yes/No chart. It looked something like this:

Did the truck leave by 9:00 am?

Date	Sept 7	Sept 8	Sept 9	Sept 10	Sept 11
Result	X	X	X	O	O

86

War on Waste Innovation

It was done on a sheet of flip chart paper and was done so that anyone passing by the area could see it. As I walked by the area with the CEO, he noticed it. He asked me what that was about. I told him that the employees had identified the importance of the truck leaving on time. If it left after 9:00 AM, it couldn't complete its rounds to the San Jose area from the North Bay and get back before the heavy commute. We looked at the chart and there were three big red X's on the chart. The red X indicates "No" in response to the posted question: Did the truck leave before 9:00 AM? So when we investigated the why of the question, it turned out that the CEO's son was not getting in on time, around 6:30 AM, to do the inspections necessary to get the parts loaded on the truck and get it out before 9:00 AM. Once the explanation was on the table, the son got in on time, the parts were inspected and the truck left before 9:00 AM. From that moment forward, the Yes/No chart had earned its merits as a valuable measuring technique.

We have used the Yes/No Chart at a number of companies to manage the truck schedule. In all of those situations, the truck rarely leaves on time, for any number of reasons. And they are usually very good reasons. Again, before the yes/no chart goes up, it must be determined that it is important that the truck leaves by a particular time. Why measure something if there are no consequences from not leaving on time? That is, if the consequences for leaving on time are no different than those for not leaving on time, this is not the right issue to measure. The individuals or departments affected by the truck's schedule must agree that a measurement is appropriate. However, once the yes/no chart goes up, all excuses are forbidden and No Blame is the rule.

When the annoyance gets large enough, things begin to change. Often, we have no idea what the causes are or what the solutions will be. It really doesn't matter, because the yes/no chart gets things moving.

We should point out here that we have not found that it is particularly effective to focus on individuals or to attempt to modify behavior directly. Rather than focusing on an individual, it is important to focus on what work is done. Additionally, it is often more useful to focus on the output of an individual's work group than on the work of that individual.

Consider these examples:

1. A worker is consistently late. A worker periodically comes late to work. It may irritate the manager that the worker is late. However, in terms of the organization's performance, the key issue is not whether the manager is irritated, but whether the team's performance is affected. If the team is affected, then we might recommend the creation of a yes/no chart to monitor this behavior. Again, the data are reported on a No Blame basis. If it is important to know this information, then it must be posted for all to see. We use the term "team" here to refer to particular work units in the business. The team may be a group, a team in all that that implies, or it may be a loose group of workers in a particular area of the business. Whatever the unit, the measurement is for the benefit of the entire team. This is an especially important point. The measurements are not for management; they are for the team, to use to improve its performance.

So, the work team makes up a yes/no chart. The question asked is: "Was everyone on the team on time today?" (yes/no) If anyone is one minute late, the report for the whole team is logged on the chart as a "No". One minute late or one hour late, the log shows a "No." The "yes/no" chart is unforgiving, because there's no room for excuses. But, we have found that most workers don't have a problem with this method of

War on Waste Innovation

measurement. Workers are usually fair to each other, and they don't like it when someone takes advantage of a situation. This approach to measurement is something we have found that they like; it is fair. The results might look like:

Was anyone late today?

	Monday	Tuesday	Wednes-day	Thursday	Friday
Yes = O No = X	X	X	X	X	O

If you want it to look very striking, put the "X's" in red and the "O's" in Green.

Managers find that the "yes/no" chart is a valuable tool. It really serves to monitor the behavior of the team. It creates the behavior that the manager would like to have, namely, that everyone is at work on time. But that behavior cannot be created until everyone on the team of concern sees that as a problem. It may be a management concern but not a team problem. When the members of the team see it as a problem, then a "Yes/No" chart is a powerful way to measure the problem, and in measuring it, eliminate it.

As we have seen it work in situations like this, the key result of this action is that everyone in the organization sees that someone on the team is coming in late, even though no individual's name is attached to this chart. Enough "no's" and an adjustment is made by the team, not the manager. Usually, the tardy individual doesn't need to be told to change his behavior, but if the errant behavior persists, the team deals with it. The individual may receive some pointed suggestions, or

Leonard Bertain, Ph.D.

the team may hold a meeting in which the issue is raised for discussion. Action is usually quick and fair. If one worker is singled out for discipline, everyone knows the problem. Nothing is done behind closed doors. The issue is dealt with openly.

The "No Blame" philosophy has a corollary: "No Excuses". In other words, no excuses are required or even accepted. Either you can get to work or you can't. Members of the team have been known to deal with the situation by volunteering to be alarm clocks for the person. They may even buy him/her an alarm clock and donate it to the cause. In other words, the "yes/no" chart puts the problem in front of everyone to see and then forces the team to deal with it when inappropriate behavior appears.

Obviously, there can be managerial concern about the "yes/no" Chart. If some of the control (measuring and then adjusting) is now in the hands of the work team, then there is less need for supervision to make decisions about the work. Then what does a supervisor or manager do with the time previously spent controlling the work (and the workers)? This is a realistic concern, but if the manager is truly concerned about work performance, what difference does it make in how it is accomplished? Now the supervisor or manager can devote time to another high priority issue. When our clients find this is an issue, we routinely see that they redirect supervisory personnel to such activities as coaching, facilitating, teaching, expediting, project work, etc. All of these activities are performed as a service to the value-adding activities carried out by their former supervisees.

It is our belief that: **Measurement is intended to improve the output of the organization, not the control of the manager. Measurement is thus a tool for the workers, not**

the managers. This doesn't mean that managers can't know what the measures are; it's just not their primary job to use the measurements to adjust performance. Leave that to the workers, be aware of their efforts to adjust performance, and help if you're asked.

2. <u>Company Can't Ship Orders on Time:</u> A small company had a long-standing and costly problem; it couldn't manage to ship orders on time. The cause of the problem boiled down to a major disagreement between individuals in different departments about what constituted an order and who could make a commitment to ship by a particular date. Most problem behavior revolved around this issue.

We discussed the problem with the client, and settled on using the yes/no chart as the means to attack the problem. The chart asked a simple question: "Were all orders shipped on time?" The results were reported by the person most likely to have the information, the guy on the shipping dock; he knew what had been shipped. The President promised a pizza party for everyone if they shipped all the orders (usually between 200 and 350) on time. A simple chart was prepared, and "no's" were recorded for fourteen days in a row. However, on the fifteenth day, a "yes" appeared, indicating shipping success! (See following chart!)

The President should have been happy about this. He had to buy pizza when they succeeded. He didn't mind that but he suspected something was wrong. He investigated and found out that the guy on the shipping dock had shipped 310 orders on time. One of the last few items was going to be 5 days late. So he made it 6 days late by shipping it on Monday.

Did all orders ship on time?

8-Sep	9-Sep	10-Sep	11-Sep	12-Sep	15-Sep	16-Sep	17-Sep	18-Sep	19-Sep	Totals
X	X	X	X	X	X	X	X	X	X	**0**
22-Sep	23-Sep	24-Sep	25-Sep	26-Sep	29-Sep	30-Sep	1-Oct	2-Oct	3-Oct	
X	X	X	X	O	X	X	O	O	O	**4**
6-Oct	7-Oct	8-Oct	9-Oct	10-Oct	13-Oct	14-Oct	15-Oct	16-Oct	17-Oct	
X	X	O	X	X	O	O	O	O	O	**6**

The President laughed because the employees had won. But he raised the bar, pizza only happened with 3 days in a row to get around the earlier problem. On the next Friday, they won again. He raised the bar to earn pizza to 5 days in a row and the employees got it after the 6th week. From that point forward they didn't have a missed shipment for 8 months. This example drives home the main message of our measurement philosophy: **Measure the problem. Measure it simply. Post it for all to see.** In the example just cited, no one, including the president, expected a "yes" to appear for several months. After all, the problem had been around for years. The fact that the "yes's" began on the fifteenth day was more than encouraging; it got everybody in the company excited that they could perform as a team to solve the problem. Everyone knew the goal of the company was to ship 100% of the orders on time. There was No Blame for failure but then again there were to be No Excuses.

As a corollary to this issue, when we begin assignments, we are often told that the company has high absenteeism, low morale, etc. We are then asked, "What are you going to do about it?" And we answer, typically, "Nothing." We don't solve problems directly; we help other people solve problems.

War on Waste Innovation

If we solve the problems, we are the ones who are learning. We want our clients to learn to learn to solve problems using our concepts. So, we assure that the burden of solving organizational problems is on the shoulders of the client employees; in our experience, they always find a way to solve the problems. In all cases, measurement is the key to solving these problems.

3. Field Plant-care Technicians - Never called in on Schedule

A final example is one of my favorites. One of our early clients was a plant care company. Each of the field Plant-care Technicians was supposed to call into the Nursery to schedule pickup of plants that needed to be delivered to their clients. These were field personnel who were out in the field taking care of plants and flowers placed in corporate facilities in a major city. These people were to call the nursery by 10:00 AM the day before their scheduled pick up day at the headquarters. In all there were 13 such technicians in the field and their calls were distributed to different days of the week.

The rules were very simple. They had to call before 10:00 AM, not 10:01 AM. The data of the first four weeks is noted in the chart below. You will note that of the 52 different calls that were to be made by 13 technicians over 4 weeks that 26/52 calls were not made on time. That is, they were late 50% of the time.

They got a red X if they didn't get to the nursery person by 10:00 AM. A number of the technicians made their calls at 9:57 AM, got through to the operator before 10:00 AM but were put on hold while the nursery manager got to the phone. By the time the manager got on the line, it was after 10:00 AM. This resulted in their failure to report on time and put an "X" on the day's results.

93

Leonard Bertain, Ph.D.

Did the plant tech call before 10:00 AM and talk to the Nursery supervisor about the next day's delivery?

Technician	1	2	3	4	5	6	7	8	9	10	11	12	13	1st 4 wks	2nd 4 wks
Week 1	X	X	O	X	X	O	O	X	X	O	X	X	X	9	
Week 2	O	X	X	O	O	X	X	X	O	X	O	O	O	6	
Week 3	X	O	O	X	O	X	O	O	X	O	X	O	X	6	
Week 4	O	X	X	O	X	O	X	X	O	O	O	O	O	5	
Week 5	O	O	O	O	O	O	O	O	O	O	O	O	O		0
Week 6	O	O	O	O	O	O	X	O	O	O	O	X	O		2
Week 7	O	O	O	O	O	O	O	O	O	O	O	O	O		0
Week 8	O	O	O	O	O	O	O	O	O	O	O	O	O		0
Total	2	3	2	2	2	2	3	3	2	2	2	2	2	26	2
Percentage Late Calls =														50%	4%

(And this all happened in the days before cell phones were available to the plant techs. They had to find phone booths or other remote phones to call in to the office.)

Guess what? The next time they called they did so with enough time to spare so that they weren't late again.

This is a very powerful tool of measurement and it generates positive results very quickly.

At the end of the month, the results of the first 4 weeks were discussed and the employees got real mad when the results showed their failures. The group had done very badly. The owner of the business went ballistic when she saw the results. They were posted every day and she just never looked at them. So one of the major things that I got from this was that if you post the results, keep tabs on them every day and provide appropriate feedback to get the results that you want. Don't wait until the end of the month. If you are playing a game, you want to know the score immediately. Posting them and then discussing them 4 weeks after the action would be

War on Waste Innovation

like a baseball scorekeeper getting in touch with a baseball player 4 weeks after a game and telling him that he lost. Who cares at that point? Make the results known immediately.

Anyway, after calming the owner down, we set a goal to improve the results and surprisingly of the 52 calls made in the next 4 weeks only 2 failed to meet the goal. Impressive? Certainly, but it is not an unusual result. It works.

"Kaizen Working in America"

One of my early experiences with measurement at companies convinced me that most systems of measurement in America are flawed. In these environments, measurement of work is based upon absolute standards of performance. For example, an assembly line worker needs to produce 50 widgets a day. That is the standard. The worker is praised at the end of the day if s/he exceeds the 50-widget objective. The problem with this scenario is that the worker may be able to produce more than the standard.[10] In such situations, in which the worker can produce more than the standard and the company wants more, we proved that we could get that performance increase by challenging the workers to compete against themselves and others. So we established the concept of a World Record Report.

The real basis of this measurement technique is the unique characteristic of Americans (see "American Management Paradox") that supports this. Americans are basically rugged individualists and are very competitive. They like to know

---

[10] There is of course the assembly line situation where there are a precise number of products that will be produced per shift. That is not what the World Record Report is used to control. The World Record Report is used when the demand exceeds capacity of a plant and processes can be improved to increase the capacity.

when they've won the game. But if the game has no winner, they won't care.

This whole process started at a company when I noticed that the workers were excited when we posted their daily performance at the end of the day. They were excited by the results. Then I challenged them to try to hit a particular performance number. It was a real stretch of their capabilities. They got excited and quickly improved their process so that the target number was easily within reach. But they never reached it. They felt confident that they could reach the number and then coasted.

When I saw that, I changed the game. I remembered my Canadian friend's comment about Americans being very competitive. So I created a game where the workers tried to break daily records. Did they perform at a level today that bested any previous performance? Now this was a fun game? They competed against themselves and they competed against other teams that were trying to break performance records in their work area. But the best part of this game, it increased profits every time a record was broken. If a record was broken, that meant that a team had improved and if it improved, it was making more money for the company. One of the interesting results of this measurement is that when a team has broken 5 or 6 world records, it has made a real breakthrough in performance. It is usually a big time profit improvement. So this leads to an explanation of how the World Record Report works.

World Record Reports

We have applied World Record Reports to manufacturing businesses, computers, processing records, picking orders in a warehouse, processing sheets and dirty wash in a laundry. We have found that World Record Reports can be applied in the four areas as noted below:

1. Set-up Time: the time required to tear down, clean up, and put away the tools of the previous job to set up the job that will be run next.

2. Run Time: the time it takes to do a job, from start to finish.

3. Quality: this is usually measured in terms of rejects or reworks on a job. Quality is also a matter of the work's conformity to customers' expectations.

4. Quantity: This is a measure of the actual output of a particular work center in one shift. Each shift should be separately accountable for production output.

All four of these measures are important in optimizing work output. Interestingly enough, we have observed that over the last 25 years, far more attention has been paid in U.S. business to quality than to set-up and run time. Perhaps this phenomenon is in part based on the focus of executives and manufacturing managers who went to Japan to study the reasons for the high quality of Japanese auto production. In an automobile plant, the set-up and run time for each job is fixed by the speed of the assembly line. There is no variability of set-up or run time on each auto. The parts just flow. Because run time and set-up time are fixed, the only variable is quality. Naturally, quality is where the Japanese focused all their attention in the production of automobiles.

It makes sense for the auto industry.

But most companies, manufacturing and service companies alike have variable product lines and need to pay attention to set- up and run time. Ideally of course, in creating the optimal

Leonard Bertain, Ph.D.

process, all set-ups are zero and all run times are minimal. As we look at work, the ideal is reasonable. It takes work, but is a worthy goal, one that we pursue with each client.

We accept as a cardinal rule of measurement that it must meet several criteria.

➡ Simple and easy to determine;

➡ Immediate;

➡ Available to the person(s) doing the work;

➡ Real.

If these criteria are met, then workers at all levels can measure their results, make timely corrections, and check to see if the corrections make a difference. We believe that everyone wants to be competent at his/her work. Once you have established measures that meet the above criteria, workers have the means to achieve a sense of their competence, and improve in accordance with that measure of competence.

The world record report evolved out of this work. In essence, the world record report is a running measure of performance that allows the worker to measure how they are doing in comparison to a "standard."

It works like this: One starts by recording the performance of that day's output. It is reported as a 100% of the goal. That performance is now the World Record. Each day's output is then compared to that number and recorded as a percentage. Whenever performance is shown to be above 100%, a new, world record has been set.

Each day's report is simply the ratio of today's performance to the world record and all figures afterward are reported in relation to the new record. Depending on the situation, one's desire may be for the numbers to get bigger or smaller. In the

98

War on Waste Innovation

case of sales, we want the sales volume to go up; the sales numbers reported should reflect that goal. However, in the case of setup time, we want it to go down. Improvement in performance will yield a smaller number; again, the numbers are reported to reflect that goal.

World Record Report

Day	1	2	3	4	5	6	7	8	9	10	11	12	13	14	15
% Output	100%	117%	101%	84%	115%	84%	90%	102%	102%	86%	84%	104%	116%	102%	97%
World Record	134	157	159	159	183	183	183	186	190	190	190	198	230	234	23
Output	134	157	159	134	183	154	165	186	190	163	160	198	230	234	22

Day	16	17	18	19	20	21	22	23	24	25	26	27	28	29	30
% Output	98%	109%	93%	100%	104%	98%	106%	89%	101%	100%	97%	105%	97%	100%	52%
World Record	234	254	254	254	265	265	280	280	282	282	282	295	295	296	29
Output	229	254	235	253	265	260	280	250	282	281	273	295	285	296	15

The above production chart from one of our clients shows a month's performance as a table of data. The world record was broken 13 times during the month (Count the number of times the % Output is over 100% - a World Record). Remember you do not break a world record when you just meet 100%. It is only when you exceed 100% that you have broken the World Record. Daily output went from a world record of 134 to a world record of 296 on the 29th day! One could argue that the net output only went up from 134 units to 154 (the output of the 30th day) over the course of the month. That's true! But the standard was raised to 296 and everybody was now into this game. And by the way, the performance on the 30th day was down because we celebrated the results. The game being played here is fun.

The workers know that they are being pushed but they don't mind it if the "No Blame" philosophy is in place.

Leonard Bertain, Ph.D.

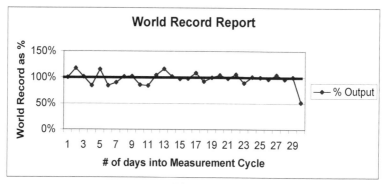

Figure 1

In Figure 1, you will notice that there is a line across the graph at the 100% point. That line is there to keep everyone focused on the goal of hitting it and after a world record is achieved to see if the output can be sustained. You will also notice that there were a lot of World Records broken in the first 15 days. As the chart is maintained, you will notice fewer and fewer world records are broken. As a manager, you need to continue to push to see if World Records can be broken. And when employees see this as an ongoing challenge, it forces them to work together to see where opportunities for improvement might be.

So, the world record report meets our criteria for measurement. It's simple. It's immediate. It's available to the people doing the work. And it's real.

It becomes a key tool that workers can use to meet their own needs for improving. By setting the "world record" as the standard keeps everyone focused on what the best work output looks like. Incidentally, the world record reports can be for an

100

War on Waste Innovation

individual, a team, a department, or a whole organization. It depends on what the relevant work unit is.

As we have discovered, the world record report is a particularly powerful form of measurement in continuous improvement environments because it shows clearly how often performance has improved. Managers should be able to visit a work area, look at the world record report, and know immediately how the work is progressing in the work area. If the workers are improving the process, it will be immediately evident. Congratulations are in order. When a manager looks at the chart and sees no improvement in a week or month, it's possible the individual or team needs help. The manager can ask what's going on. That's O.K. This is much more a question of leadership than of managing. The worker and manager can use the data on the WRR to determine whether changes are needed. This is the best use of measurement: to help improve the performance of the organization.

When we use the world record report to measure output, we are measuring value; that's our goal. We want to eliminate waste and increase value. The world record report gives us a performance measurement that tells us how we are doing in this regard. If the process is improving and we are increasing our value-adding results, then we are on the right track. At some point, however, performance improvement will slow; we'll break the world record less frequently. When this happens, we can explore whether further improvement is possible, if an investment of technology is needed, or whether we've arrived at Kansas City and "we've gone about as far as we can go."

A few examples of the application of the world record report follow:

Leonard Bertain, Ph.D.

1. Set-up Reduction Example: In one client-company, they knew that they needed to reduce the set-up time on their CNC (computerized numerical control) machines. There was no doubt in anyone's mind that their current set-up time was excessive; fully 35% of machinists' time was utilized for set-up. We began by making all the employees aware that value could only be delivered when the CNC machine was cutting metal. So, this was what was measured, the number of hours/day when the machine was actually cutting metal. At first, the measures made everyone uncomfortable. The numbers were low, very low, and since we operate on the basis of "no excuses" as well as "no blame," the numbers were reported just as they were. No complicated excuses, just the hours of actual value-added work per day.

The numbers improved.

When we worked with the employees on analyzing the set-up process, finding ways to reduce the time required to set-up, they were enthusiastic. And the set-up reduction showed up in new records on the WRR. Eventually, set-up time dropped to less than 10% of its original size. But that's another story.

The background of this set-up problem sheds some light on how measurement is part of both the problem and the solution. In a previous effort to deal with this problem, the owner had recorded set-up times. He quoted each job with a standard set-up time of 4 hours, and asked each of the machinists to report the <u>actual</u> set-up time to him. One unfortunate individual reported that a particular set-up had taken 7 hours. When the owner got that information, he hit the roof. The employee, being the alert fellow that he was, asked if he could recheck his figures. He was excused and this time he came back with the "right" numbers; set-up was only 4 hours! As we learned later, actual set-up time on this job was more in the neighborhood of

War on Waste Innovation

9 hours, not 4. Obviously, machinists had been hiding the truth all along, out of fear that it wouldn't be acceptable. They were quite correct.

So, "lesson one" in all of our work is to begin the process of reporting honest data in a "no blame" atmosphere. We believe that clients will never be able to improve if they don't know the accurate baseline data. It's just like golf; you've got to count <u>all</u> your strokes (not like me). And then you can improve your game.

In this example, the owner didn't really want to face up to the reality of how bad his operation really was. Although it was acceptable by industry standards, it was actually fairly inefficient. He didn't want to face the poor process methods for what they were because he was embarrassed. When it was suggested that the best measurement of the business was the actual spindle time spent cutting metal, he resisted this notion and argued for more complex (and more confusing) measures. Unconsciously, he was avoiding the truth. However, since each operator was cutting metal only 33% of each day, the fact is inescapable that 67% of each work day was devoted to waste. That was a bitter pill to swallow. As it turned out, the hours of cutting metal (adding value) was closer to two hours (25% of each day), when averaged over the course of a week.

It may seem obvious to anyone who has been around business organizations very long that employees would hide the truth about their performance, but it is not obvious to many CEO's. When an employee is asked to report his real operating efficiencies to anyone "above" in the organization, fear of being blamed arises. With that fear comes distortion. To overcome that fear, an atmosphere of no blame is necessary; with blaming banished, valid measurement can proceed.

Leonard Bertain, Ph.D.

2. Another example: a client was concerned about what he was going to do once teams were created and the control of factory work was in the hands of the work teams. This is a common concern that we help clients address. We helped him explore how to lead (rather than manage) and how to redirect his efforts away from the shop floor and to the external environment in which the organization existed.

His discovery: since we had, in the War on Waste process, developed a thorough understanding of the needs and priorities of the team's contributions necessary to the business, the teams took on their work without a hitch. He was surprised but pleased.

We also helped him learn the value and use of the world record report. When you examine the data presented in the accompanying chart, notice that there are a number of points that are above the 100% line (Figure 2 below). Each such point indicates that the measurement has exceeded the best performance to date.

So, a number of new "world records" have been set. That deserves attention, and from a leadership perspective, the individual or team deserves recognition. Additionally, it requires an understanding of what happened to cause the improvement, so the process can be continually enhanced.

War on Waste Innovation

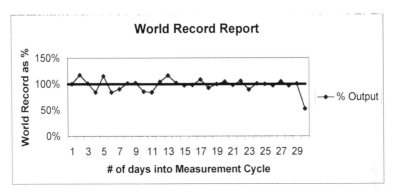

Figure 2

When the world record is broken, that's a cause for celebration. When the improvement over the previous WR is large, say 15%, this is probably significant. If this occurs some months into the process, it is definitely significant, and means that something important has happened. We encourage managers to pay attention to this immediately so that it happens again and is not a one-time occurrence. In many of my clients, a big order comes in. Everybody in the organization gets focused to deliver the order on time. And in the frenzy of the day, set-up times go down and production goes through the roof. Now the question is, why? Can we make that level of performance an everyday occurrence?

For the leader to help the system sustain these significant changes is very important. If the changes are sustained, the results of the following days will be reflected in the output of the work unit immediately following the breaking of a world record. A one-time occurrence looks like figure 3.

105

Leonard Bertain, Ph.D.

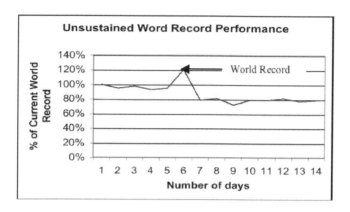

Figure 3

A sustained process might look like Figure 4.

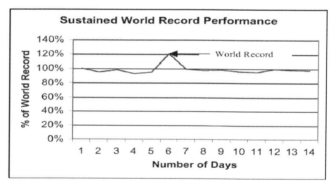

Figure 4

Whatever the reason for the change, information reported in this way is a very powerful tool and is important in an environment of continuous-improvement. This is considered an un-sustained world record (Figure 3) because after the world record was established the production was not able to sustain it. You can see that the performance indicators return to about 80% of the world record. This means that the process improved but was not sustainable. In Figure 4, the world

106

War on Waste Innovation

record is set and the performance of the operation responds by being able to sustain the performance improvement. The performance is sustained because the on going daily indicators show performance is maintaining around the 100% mark.

Any member of the organization can easily learn how to read and use the WRR's. They tell employees what is needed to focus the resources to help a team. If, for instance, the one-time success occurs, it is important to understand why the improvement was only one-time. Was there some extenuating circumstance to cause the improvement? If so, what was it? Can it be repeated to make it happen again? These are all part of the questioning process that must occur as these reports are interpreted. Resetting the World Record Report to a zero point, the "100%" line, makes it easy to see when something significant happens in the process. Once seen, it can then be analyzed.

Tribal Knowledge Council (TKC)

The paradigm requires a formal process to get new ideas into the system. Once there, they need to be tracked and implemented. That is achieved with the Tribal Knowledge Council.

The TKC is the control point for the input of all ideas. Its purpose is to be the clearing-house for change and new ideas. It serves as a touchstone for the CEO and his Executive team. They use it to keep track of ideas as they move through the system.

It is not managed as much as it is a monitor. It is an automated function with a dashboard. The dashboard tracks the progress of results.

A word of caution here: this council has no direct authority. Nor should it. It merely facilitates the process of putting ideas into play. If authority is given, it will create two problems. One, it will conflict with line management authority. And two, it will create an artificial elite status. This will dampen participation.

The Japanese call this "Kaizen." It is continuous improvement. For them, ongoing innovation does not occur by chance. It is part of their national religion. It is Zen Buddhism's strive for perfection. But as we noted earlier, this concept rolls off American Managers. If it is framed in terms of Internal Growth or profit improvement, it definitely rings the bell. We learned this early in the War on Waste.

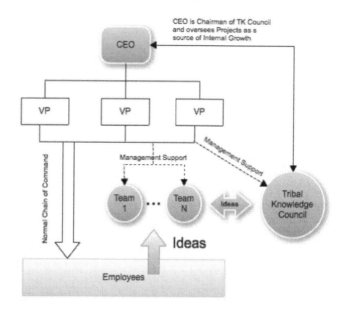

War on Waste Innovation

The TKC reports to the CEO as noted in the chart above. As shown, all ideas to improve are routed through the TKC.

In this diagram, the CEO is the Chairman of the TKC. It isn't necessary for the CEO to attend all or any of the meetings. The CEO just needs to see the input, progress and output of the ideas going in. The TKC is ideally automated in large companies. However, it is not a complicated process. And so, for small companies, it can be manual. Fortune 100 companies have a larger volume of ideas. So it is best to automate that process.

A few words need to be said about the staffing of the TKC. It cannot become a place for anyone to create an agenda of power. The TKC is merely where ideas go. They are tracked from initiation of the idea to the proposed solution. It is tracked and reported for all to see.

The TKC tracks the increase of revenue or cost reduction projected by a team. The CEO and the Executive Team keep in touch with the results. Successful teams will be recognized. That will happen both when the idea is ready to go and when an idea hits its target.

We had a concern about making the TKC a power position. At first glance, it could be a great starting point for a young manager. It could be a great way to meet everyone in the company. However, we had observed a problem with this in other venues. When we tried to create "idea centers", we saw it often. A well-meaning employee would get into the position and problems arose. Their personal agenda would come into play. Tension would lead to conflicts with front line supervisors. Time demands to work on a project took away from value-added work. This created the tension. So we noted the best way to avoid that problem was to take away the option. So we insist that CEOs instruct the TKC head to keep the ideas

Leonard Bertain, Ph.D.

flowing. Keep the CEO abreast of great new ideas. And push all suggested ideas to completion.

Ideally in the Tribal Knowledge Paradigm ideas flow from every employee. In this methodology, improving Tribal Knowledge is a defined responsibility of every manager. That objective was defined to be the second of the Tribal Knowledge Paradigm principles. By making this a key tenet, we have avoided the tension. Instead, we have directed the same managers to support new ideas. Now, that is their job.

One of the most difficult parts of this process in large companies is dealing with lawyers. In most Fortune 500 companies, there is a patent or IP group. This group sometimes gets involved. They ask (demand) to look over the shoulder of the TKC activities. They want to make sure that ideas with patent potential are identified early. That way they insure IP is protected.

On the other hand, these groups are by nature power centers. They need to be controlled as well. With a "power hungry" patent monitoring lawyer, nothing would get done. All ideas would be scrutinized with a fine-toothed comb. Progress would grind to a halt. This is normal in the balance of innovation and IP protection. It is not a danger, merely a precaution. We encourage this conflict because it is important. The lawyers need to be guided because they can be useful (imagine that).

The tracking of all ideas is the responsibility of the TKC. Implementation is the responsibility of the team. When managers get involved, they provide support. So when someone has an idea for a process improvement, the idea is submitted. A problem solving structure is applied to get the idea converted into action. The implementation plan and metrics of success are posted for all to see. The progress of the team is posted by the TKC or is available on line.

The TKC is the Single Point of Tracking for all ideas and innovations. These are ideas that improve Mission Relevant Tribal Knowledge in the company. All ideas, large and small need to be reported here. The ideas serve as the basis of what was noted earlier with "earned" recognition. We know that some ideas are very easy to implement. They usually don't get much attention. But as we noted earlier, the idea is important. And all ideas need to be respected. We respect even the small ideas. This is important because even these ideas help the cash flow.

"Respect ideas!" That is the foundation of the Tribal Knowledge Paradigm.

Moment of Truth (MOT)

This is an encounter between a customer and a business. This can be in person, over the telephone, over the Internet or any other way business is transacted. Each such encounter leads to a "Moment of Truth." And the experience can be either good or bad. Jan Carlzon, former CEO of SAS Airlines, noted in his book, "Moments of Truth."[11] There were over 50,000 daily encounters with customers at his airline when every passenger or phone call contact is defined as a Moment of Truth. He reasoned that since he couldn't be present for every MOT, his company had to be totally customer focused.

What is the difference between the 50,000 daily MOT's at SAS Airline and the 70,000 web-site hits processed by an

---

[11] Carlzon, Jan "Moments of Truth" Harper and Row, New York, 1987

Leonard Bertain, Ph.D.

Internet site? Nothing!!! In each case, a Moment of Truth is a one-on-one experience. If a visit to the web site is confusing and difficult to navigate, visitors will leave and won't come back. If you get it right, the customer will come back.

In most scenarios, business is pretty simple. For example, a customer is looking for a product and your business has the needed product. The customer calls and you sell it to him or her. If the result of that experience is good, it will fulfill the user's needs, either in the form of a buying experience or in the extraction of information. But it doesn't always work that way. Sometimes the customer is not pleased by the experience with your company and that leads to a negative moment of truth. And this customer will probably not return.

Business today is full of companies that have had to redefine themselves by the changes demanded by the New Economy. The Moment of Truth concept forces a business to examine its commitment to being customer focused. If all Moments of Truth are positive, then a return visit from the customer is almost assured.

I used to shop at Safeway Stores before they made a major change in how their employees interacted with customers. I hated to shop there. The employees were nasty. But they trained all employees to recognize the importance of the customer. It really worked. Now when I go to Safeway Stores, every Moment of Truth is extremely positive. I just love to go there. I remember the first time that I returned to the store after the change had occurred and I needed some cheese. I asked where the cheese is located. The employee dropped what she was doing and not only told me where it was but she took me there.

Now, every time that I need to ask for help, the employees will drop whatever they are doing to walk me over to the appropriate section of the store. Once I get there, they always ask if I need anything else. I like to tell about this because in my past experiences it was not always pleasant to go to Safeway. Trust me, when employees understand the value of making all Moments of Truth positive good things will happen, like more profits.

Multiple Points of Control

Multiple Points of Control is a waste that occurs when more than one person is involved in making a decision regarding a business process. In one War on Waste project, a team had identified a waste that occurred when a product was committed to ship to a customer by the salesmen or managers to customers based upon what the computer said was in inventory. Of course, the computer was wrong most of the time. So to check things out, whoever was taking an order on a part with low inventory would go out to the warehouse and verify inventory status. That worked well if no one else wanted the same item. A waste occurred because on 50% of the orders of 5 or more items, at least two people were claiming the same item. So when they committed to a customer a specific ship date for the order, at least one of the orders was going to be late.

Of course, the obvious fix was to get inventory control software that worked. We didn't have time to do that during the War on Waste so we solved the problem by creating a single point of control. Instead of having multiple people (multiple points of control) making decisions about what inventory was going to be committed to specific orders, the team decided to make one person the control point. That way, when an order was committed for a particular date, it stuck. Within 6 weeks, all orders were shipping on time.

Leonard Bertain, Ph.D.

So when we identify a waste with a root cause of Multiple Points of Control, the solution is a "Single Point of Control."

Five (5) Why's

Taichi Ohno was the developer of the Toyota Production System. As such he was the father of manufacturing Just in Time systems. One of his great ideas was a technique that he developed (The Five Whys) to get to the root cause of a problem. It goes something like this.

When someone identifies a problem, you ask the question "why did that happen?" five times and you are almost guaranteed to get to the root cause by the fifth why. As an example, if a worker comes into a business owner in a panic and tells him that a fellow worker fell and is being taken to the hospital to treat a broken arm, the owner would of course show concern about the injured worker. His next concern would be how the accident occurred. So he asks the obvious question: "Why did he fall?" (First Why!) The employee answers, "Because he tripped on an air line." The CEO asks again, "Why was the air line on the floor?" (Second Why!) The employee replies, "Because there was no air line outlet on that side of the aisle." So the CEO says, "then let's put an air line outlet on the other side of the aisle." The root cause was found after the second "Why."

As another example, nurses and doctors were looking into the cycle time for a surgery. The cycle time is the time from when the patient left the hospital room until s/he returned to the bed in ICU. So we asked why it took so long? Because the patient waited outside the surgery room until it was cleaned up. Why was he waiting for the room to be cleaned up? Answer: because there were only two technicians cleaning up the room. Why were there only two? The hospital had not trained enough prep and cleanup technicians. The solution: train more techs. The root cause was found after the third why. The waste: revenue lost per hour versus the cost of paying two more techs to clean the room and speed the surgery room turnover.

Tribal Knowledge Council - Manage Kaizen

One of the questions that I get asked all the time is how do you sustain change? Or better yet, how do you continue to get new ideas into the system and get them implemented? After the training is complete, we introduce client employees to the problem-solving set-up, that we call the Tribal Knowledge Council (TKC). The TKC is the control point for managing innovation in the business. The purpose of the TKC, as discussed earlier, is to be the clearing-house for change or new ideas for improvement.

In the Tribal Knowledge Paradigm, managers and executives support the Tribal Knowledge Council by making sure that all ideas from their subordinates are routed through the TKC. In that way, they are assured that they are doing their job by improving Tribal Knowledge or Know How.

The Japanese call this continuous process improvement activity "Kaizen".

Continuous improvement and ongoing innovation is not an accidental discovery; it is part of their national religion, Zen Buddhism. The philosophy of Zen is reflected in the quote of Konushuke Matsushita (see "Matsushita" Page 21).

In the Tribal Knowledge Paradigm, the TKC reports to the CEO as noted in the chart below. All innovation ideas are routed through the TKC. The key to the operation of the TKC is that it is staffed with non-Executive personnel.

Leonard Bertain, Ph.D.

Tribal Knowledge Council

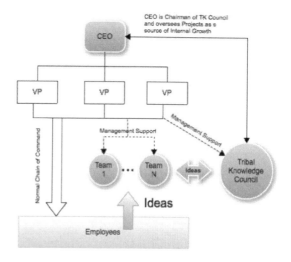

One of the major complaints that I've heard about the TKC is that the process for implementing policy change through such a board is going to make the process very slow. I would probably agree with that idea superficially but you have to look at the length of time that it takes for the policy to not only get started but to be put into practice. As an example of this, in one of my clients, the head of Engineering had to leave town on a business trip. He had a new RMA (Return Materials Authorization)[12] policy that he wanted to implement. So he hurriedly wrote the policy, bounced it off a few of his peers, and sent it out to all managers for implementation.

---

[12] An RMA is a Return Material Authorization. In a company that sells a product that can be returned for repair or replacement, an RMA document, or something like it, is required from sales or whomever to activate the process of repair or replacement. Sounds easy but evidence is overwhelming that it isn't.

War on Waste Innovation

As he headed out the door, I told him that he should run this policy through the TKC. He couldn't be bothered and the CEO was not around to intervene. Besides he said, the process would take too long. I thought a second and told him that when he got back from his trip we would check to see if his policy had been successfully implemented. He agreed to meet with me and on his return 2 weeks later and I was there waiting for him. We walked out to the RMA area and asked the technician in charge of evaluating RMA's whether he had seen the new RMA policy. He thought that he had. Then he reached into his file drawer and pulled it out. Of course, he had received it. That wasn't too surprising. But when we found that over 50% of the employees that had a need to know had never seen the policy, it was clear that the old way wasn't working.

So we turned the new RMA policy over to the TKC. They convened a meeting, picked a team of 4 employees from departments that might be concerned with a new RMA policy. They took the proposed policy and walked it around the company and got input from a number of employees. The policy was revised and then passed by all department directors. Unanimous approval was obtained and all of this only took 3 days and about 10 total man-hours of effort. The new policy was submitted to the CEO for approval. A new survey, at the end of 1 week indicated that everyone knew the new RMA policy and that was that.

One of the concepts that we discovered is that once the TKC gets rolling, all ideas don't need to be routed through the TKC. If an idea doesn't affect any other department, that we call a class 1 problem, then we set up a budget for each department to insure that class 1 problems (class 2 problems - only 2 departments; class 3 problems - more than 2 departments) get solved. If you try this first, when the TKC is

117

Leonard Bertain, Ph.D.

set up, you may end up with a problem. Many of the best ideas come from employees who work for a manager or leader who is threatened by employee ideas and they never get a consideration from the manager. For this reason, it is recommended that all ideas get routed through the TKC. Then, if it should be handled in a department, it is coordinated by the TKC, that is supported by the CEO. I know that when we have the problem routed back to the department and the CEO supports the TKC activity, things get done. Until the process gets working correctly, it usually works best to rout all ideas through the TKC.

In classifying problems, a class 1 problem is one that only effects a single department, like a process improvement issue. You have to be careful because some process improvement issues can be class 3 problems because they affect the quality department, product engineering, manufacturing engineering, purchasing, and so on. You have to really think through the classification of a problem. A class 2 problem is one that only effects 2 departments, no more than 2. All other problems are class 3 problems.

Consider the following examples: if you want to change a data input screen to make it more efficient, it is usually a class 3 problem because more than 2 departments are affected by this change. If you want to improve the purchasing process, it usually affects at least 3 departments (purchasing, manufacturing and administration). As you work through this classification process, you will soon get the hang of it.

The TKC is the Single Point of Control for all innovation in the company. We have sample charters and by-laws of the TKC. If you email me at the address below, you can get a copy of them in electronic format. They have been revised a number of times but I believe that each company should write its own

War on Waste Innovation

and edit them as needed to deal with conditions specific to its business. You may email me at len@bertain.com.

Report Honest Data

As you might guess, the whole concept of measurement is based on reporting honest data. But sometimes it isn't possible. At one of our early clients, a work cell was created to manufacture the particular product of interest and the workers were asked to report the output of the cell each day and post it for all to see. Everyone in the shop knew the daily production output of this cell. It was reported on a continuous basis in big, bold numbers on a white board, totally visible to all employees.

Several weeks later, the owner noticed that the numbers were down from the previous day. He immediately jumped on the lead man in the work area, since he knew only one way to deal with problems: confrontation. The owner didn't fully appreciate that in the War on Waste approach the concept of NO BLAME is an underpinning philosophy. We reminded him and he retraced his steps and apologized to the lead man.

His actions, however, gave us the idea for a different way to measure. We wanted an approach that would be based on a No Blame philosophy, wouldn't point fingers, and yet would measure critical variables that we wanted to influence. But we wanted "Honest Data." The "No Blame" concept is the basis of War on Waste's measurement process. 'No Blame" and simplicity of measurement are the important ingredients of this process, as we lead our clients toward improved productivity. There is a key linkage between "No Blame" and "Reporting of Honest Data;" they go hand in hand. We often initiate discussion of the importance of honest data by showing a vignette from "History of the World: Part 2". As you may recall, Moses (played by Mel Brooks) comes down from the mountain holding 3 tablets, and he speaks to the children of

119

Leonard Bertain, Ph.D.

Israel, saying: "I bring you the fifteen..." Just then, he drops one of the tablets and exclaims: "Oy!" He then begins again. "I bring you the Ten Commandments." This really makes our point about reporting of honest data. And it had a little humor as well.

War on Waste Innovation

Change Issues

WOW is all about creating a changed work environment. To create this change, there are a lot of issues that need to be addressed. We try to understand how those issues can influence the resulting company of our efforts. Black Knights, for example, are hindrances to the change process. If you want to improve a business and survive in today's competitive world you had better know about change.

Leonard Bertain, Ph.D.

Change - Three Keys to Change

"Plus ca change, plus ca meme change, non!"
The more it changes, the more it remains the same.

I have been an advocate of change that leads to business improvement for a long time. Some people have called me a "Change agent". For a long time, I liked that term. Then one day, after I had worked with a particular CEO for over 2 years, I realized that I was no longer the agent of change, I had become a pain in the ass for this client. At first I was welcomed with open arms. As time progressed, my ideas had found their way into the culture of the company and a new paradigm was created within the company. I had served my purpose.

After this particular CEO had gotten a two-year dose of my change ideas, he didn't want me around. I don't think he was mad at me. He was mad at what I represented. I represented change. I was the "change agent." This particular CEO knew that when he saw me that I was going to have another idea to improve his business. Each new idea made him money. But he was getting tired of the change. He had not gotten my message that if he wanted to succeed in business that he was going to have to live with change. That is the way of business.

I never understood him. I was helping him make money and he was making lots of it, but he got tired of having to continually change what he was doing. But I had missed "IT" as well. There is only one "Change Agent" in a company and that is the CEO. The CEO is in charge of change. In fact, we define the management of change to be one of the responsibilities of every CEO. It cannot be assigned or delegated. It is the CEO's job. My problem was that I didn't understand that earlier. I thought that the change agent should be someone from outside. No wonder the CEO got mad at me,

War on Waste Innovation

I had tried to take his job. This CEO knew that something wasn't right. And so we corrected it by terminating my services with his company.

To be a CEO in today's world, you had better get used to it because the good old days are going to be 6 months ago. It really takes guts to be a CEO when you live in today's world of the global economy. A product may originate in Germany, be developed in California, and be mass-produced in Malaysia. The exciting part of that equation is that the whole process only took 7 months to materialize the idea and take it to full production, in three steps, across 3 continents.

The CEO of this discussion was helpful in defining the issues that led to the Tribal Knowledge Paradigm. His resistance to change was based on my being a forcing function of change. I thought that I was being righteous in my push for change. But what this situation showed me was that I couldn't be the "Face of Change." I had to be a mentor. I couldn't lead the charge, the CEO needed to. So when we figured out that the Tribal Knowledge Paradigm was centered on the CEO's commitment to make improvement of Tribal Knowledge a touchstone of management that the change programs worked. They worked because I wasn't leading the charge, the CEO was and got all managers involved in the process. In fact, getting all managers to help the CEO is one of the foundation principles of the Tribal Knowledge Paradigm.

So in this paradigm, change is ongoing. It is a way of life, as it should be. Ideas for improving Tribal Knowledge are sacred and must be treated as such. They go to the Tribal Knowledge Council for a hearing and blessing if appropriate and change goes on.

That's the way it should be.

Leonard Bertain, Ph.D.

The Need to Change

All of the management gurus of the last 50 years have advocated various forms of change agency. But before we comment about those forms of change, I would like to comment about a more basic issue and that is the need to change.

Change is a given in business.

1. The products that you announce today are coming at you tomorrow from unscrupulous overseas competitors who steal product designs and come into your market with your own designs. So you have to respond in some way if litigation and patent infringement are not options. You have to change the way and the speed with which you introduce new products. That alone will require a change in your business.

2. World economies are changing. The exchange rate of the dollar in the international arena has a positive or negative effect on the attractiveness of your products in the global markets. You have to respond. Change in costs of the product need to be aggressively pursued. You need to change your tactics and even your strategies to survive.

3. Every solution that you come up with for any business problem today is going to create problems tomorrow for the simple reason that the logic and the reasons that guided your solution just 6 months ago are no longer valid. You need another solution. You need to change.

The 3 Keys to Change

When you look at what you need to do to change, consider these three guides. These conditions have to be met before change is possible.

War on Waste Innovation

The keys are:

* Ability to change;

* Willingness to change;

* The system that support change – policies, procedures, etc.

1. Ability

I remember one of my clients was exasperated with his employees. He wanted to implement a new computerized MRP (Material Requirements Planning) information system. He brought the employees into a room and spent about 45 minutes with them telling them about the system. They had no hands on experience and he sent them out to interact with this very complex computer system. Mind you, the concepts are very simple if you have had time to study them. It turned out that this particular CEO didn't know much about MRP systems before he spent about 6 months investigating them. From my perspective, he and his Inventory Control Manager had made a wise selection of MRP software. The CEO and his Inventory Control Manager knew the system. But it takes more than 45 minutes to expect employees to understand the intricacies of an MRP system.

Needless to say, the employees didn't have the knowledge or the ability to understand the new system and so change was going to be difficult and slow.

I could have chosen a number of examples from probably every client that I have ever had and pointed out a failure of a change project because the participants in the change didn't have the ability to change. They really didn't know enough to make the change a lasting process.

In order to do anything successfully, one must possess the ability to do it. So, to allow an individual to perform a new job

Leonard Bertain, Ph.D.

or task, we must provide him/her with knowledge, skill, or capability. Typically, we do this by providing training. Clearly, there is no point in asking anyone to do a job for which he/she lacks these tools. Neither desire nor management pressure can assure successful change. For employees to perform differently, managers must be certain that the employees can do the work. And the only way to guarantee that is to insure their ability to do the work is through education.

2. Willingness

I don't know how many times that I've said this but if you don't want to change, I can't do anything about that. Willingness to change is an individual's commitment to himself and no one else. If you don't want to change, I can't help you. I can show you all the reasons that the final result of the change is something that you should want but if you don't buy into that then I can guarantee that change will not occur. Just look at weight loss programs.

Even as one needs ability to do a given job or task, one needs to be willing to apply that ability. Very often, the ability is present, but the willingness is not. Therefore the desired behavior does not occur. Willingness in an organization may come from many quarters: for example, from an understanding of what is desired or desirable, from peer support, or from our value systems.

Thus, if you do not believe that your boss truly desires that you take on a certain behavior, you will probably not do so. Additionally, if there is no understanding of why that behavior is important or how it might affect the organization's goals, the employee might not make the desired behavioral change. It is also possible that one's peers, social group, or union might "disapprove" of taking on the change in behavior, task, or role.

War on Waste Innovation

This could lead to the individual's failure to use his ability. Organization history is full of stories of employees restricting output due to peer pressure against "rate-busters" and "company men."

Employees might also have values that prohibit engaging in desired behavior. For example, an OSHA inspector might deem it desirable for the cowboys on a ranch to wear safety equipment such as hard hats, and there is little question that the cowboys have the ability to wear hard hats. But would they? That isn't likely. It would conflict with a value system that holds cowboy hats, not hard hats, are essential to ranch work.[13]

3. The Systems that Support Change

I laugh every time that I think back at one company executive. He actually said this to me, "I don't care if every body else's job changes, stay away from mine." Boy if anyone ever gave me a red cape to charge, this guy did. So of course I charged. In fact, he turned out to be very easy to change because the changes that came up in our process made his job easier.

I don't go into companies to implement changes that make peoples jobs harder. I fully expect to change some jobs. And when I do, I fully expect them to stick. Most do, some don't. But these resistors in the system are clever. We call them "Black Knights." They control information and they don't want to give that up. They control company policy and feel that they are far better at making the decisions about rules than the uninformed line workers. They are the manipulators of Tribal Knowledge. Of course, the workers are uninformed

---

[13] I wrote this and then I saw a rodeo, Brahma bull contest, and one of the cowboys had a helmet on. Forgive my literary license in the example.

because they don't have the information needed. And that happens because the controllers of the system make sure that they are in control of all information.

So in order to change, the systems need to be in place to support change. The systems and people that control the systems need to be in favor of the changes. One CEO made it very clear to several resistors of change. He told them, "I am the General leading a War on Waste. You may be committing treason with your resistance to my changes. Decide now whether you stand with me or against me. If you resist these changes, then you have committed treason." I was a believer and so were all of his resistors. They all elected to stand with him. And the change was successful.

Concluding Thoughts

As a conclusion on change I offer this comment from Lawrence Bossidy[14], "if you focus on the customer, the employees will know that change is necessary." And I would add, "not only will they know that change is necessary, they will know what change is necessary."

Black Knights

You may remember Monty Python's "Search for the Holy Grail". In the movie, there is a scene in which a Black Knight is defending a bridge. As King Arthur approaches, the Black Knight is engaged in battle with another knight. Of course, the Black Knight wins, (he always wins!) After the defeated knight is dispatched (killed), King Arthur approaches and beseeches the Black Knight to join him at Camelot. Instead,

---

[14] Lawrence Bossidy was the CEO of Allied Signal and prior to that he was a senior level executive who worked for Jack Welch, former CEO of GE.

War on Waste Innovation

the Black Knight challenges King Arthur to a duel when Arthur tries to cross the bridge.

The Black Knight is defending the bridge, but in truth, King Arthur could easily jump across the creek. It is just a trickle. But King Arthur and the Black Knight engage in combat and the Black Knight loses an arm. When the King challenges him to give up the fight, the Black Knight denies that he has a problem. "I've had worse," he moans.

King Arthur chastises him, "Look you bastard, you don't have an arm." The Black Knight continues his denial all the way to the point where he doesn't have any arms or legs. King Arthur, ever the gallant victor, opines, "OK, we'll call it a draw."

Obviously the Black Knight was defending a stupid position. In our view of business, managers and employees at all levels of business do that. But King Arthur is just as guilty as the Black Knight. He didn't really need to challenge the Black Knight. He could have jumped across the creek and been on his way to Camelot. But Managers and plenty of executives sometimes do just that. They get into their employee's face and force a person to defend a ridiculous position.

We see the Black Knight all the time in a typical classroom session of the War on Waste.

For example, an employee might identify a waste that is a problem with one of the department managers. The manager, foreman or supervisor (The Black Knight) denies in public that the identified problem exists. So you might say that a "situation" has developed. The employee is safe hiding behind a shield of "No Blame," the manager is in denial, and the facilitator is in the middle. This looks like mission impossible.

Leonard Bertain, Ph.D.

What does the facilitator do? No matter what, you have to uphold order. But let's assume you already said that you wanted to improve the business processes and that you have signed on to the "No Blame" philosophy.

You don't need to lose points with either employee. The general rule of War on Waste is "focus on the work." The issue here isn't whether there is a Black Knight in the room or not. The issue is, "what is the right work?" If an employee has a suggestion that identifies a waste in the business, the facilitator needs to defend the employee until enough facts have been collected to substantiate the size of the waste. You need to determine how much money is wasted by the identified problem. You need to determine how much value is being lost.

This is the scientific principle at work. Find out how big a problem this is, and then see if it can still be denied as a problem when the evidence is in.

In one client, the "Black Knight" tried to derail a project that his team had decided to work on for their War on Waste presentation. He didn't want to work on it because it addressed the issue of employee turnover of which he was the major cause. The employees were all aware that he was a "Black Knight." But at some point, he realized that he needed to get on board the "Change Wagon". He did and has become a strong member of the ongoing effort to improve the business. He was a Black Knight who changed. It is possible, you know.

Boundaries

In Physics, a boundary is the physical point of separation between two or more materials--air and water, water and ice, solid and vacuum or various other combinations. All the good stuff happens at boundaries. Electromagnetic radiation, light and shock waves have clearly defined behavior inside a

War on Waste Innovation

medium. For example, light travels at a particular speed in a vacuum. When light hits water at a boundary then reflection, refraction, and polarization all happen simultaneously. Why it behaves the way makes for exciting research.

In a business, a boundary is the border between two departments. It is usually the point of transfer of information or materials that lead to "great" opportunities for wasteful things to happen. For example, what happens when the sales department hands a sales order to the inventory management people and (hopefully!) the same order to the factory?

For example, think of the following scenario. A customer gives an order to a sales manager fully expecting the products to be shipped according to the schedule. Imagine that the Sales manager drops off the order in the sales department and he is expecting that it will get processed according to the customers expectations. (What a thought!!!) He quickly fills out the order in the computer but leaves off a few key order parameters. He keys in the wrong ship date, and the product specifications are inconsistent. The wrong ship date is 3 weeks after it is really due. The Sales Manager leaves for Europe on vacation and the trusty order entry person is gone. Now the fun begins. The customer calls with a change. No one is available but someone in purchasing decides to handle the deal. Now we have two boundaries involved: the sales and manufacturing boundary and an unnecessary boundary to purchasing.

I don't need to finish the story. Everyone knows what it is about. It's an accident waiting to happen. In my view, it is at these boundaries that the fun occurs in a War on Waste project. This interaction of departments at their boundaries is where a lot of the waste in a business occurs. It is usually fertile ground for War on Waste projects. In leading the War on Waste, we look for waste at department boundaries because it can usually

131

Leonard Bertain, Ph.D.

lead to a bigger problem. Also there are often lots of "blame" at boundaries because the two sides of the boundary work for different bosses, and like good "Black Knights," employees protect their department no matter what.

Another use of the word boundary in business defines how far a person can go in performing his or her job. The size of the boundary is a measure of the freedom that a person has within a company. A person who is free to do whatever in his/her job is considered to have an open boundary or free roam of the company. This is all part of the process that I call "Chalking the Field." We discussed this earlier. It is how we define boundaries. A small boundary refers to someone who is "on a short rope" and is being closely managed. Related to the size of the employee boundary is how clearly a manager defines the boundaries of those reporting to him or her. It is probably a human trait that most of us sense the need to be accountable for our actions. We usually call it "knowing our limits." So a boundary defines our limits.

There was an experiment performed a number of years ago in which children were placed in a field without a fence. The children bunched together in the middle of the field. The researchers then put up a fence, and the children spread out. Many explored the fence and what its limits were. They tested the fence, and some even tried to climb over it.

This applies to business as well. If you define clear boundaries for employees, you will get greater use of assets. There will be greater exploration of the opportunities within the boundaries, and you will gradually be able to expand the defined boundaries as the territory becomes fully explored. New markets, new products, new personnel, and new competitors will open up the boundaries.

War on Waste Innovation

The value of defining clear boundaries is that you don't need to tell people what to do so often. You tell them where the boundary is. And you tell them what not to do. This is like defining an out in baseball. Once you know the rules, you can play the game. You encourage innovation and creativity but within loosely but clearly defined limits.

Kaizen

Tribal Knowledge needs to be improved. Making that happen is every manager's job. It must be ingrained into their thinking about how they manage. In other words, it must become a process. It is not an initiative. It is not a one-time event. It must become part of how executives, managers and supervisors manage. They will then be measured in their performance reviews by how well they do this.

It is a form of continuous improvement. But it has a different slant. The Japanese coined the term "Kaizen" to define the issue of continuous improvement. But that just bounces off American managers. It is a Zen philosophy. The Japanese have no trouble incorporating that thinking into their management philosophy.

But a different tact is needed for US Managers. They know that Tribal Knowledge and Know How are intangible assets. By focusing on them, we were helping companies send a message to shareholders that Know How is important. Managers understand that. They also know that if they improve Tribal Knowledge they are increasing shareholder value. Shareholders realize the value of Tribal Knowledge is setting the stage for Internal Growth opportunities. And managers can really get behind this.

To the Japanese and to an American, it is exciting to make any improvement in the work process. For instance, if a set-up on a particular process is reduced from 4 hours to 1 hour that is exciting. And when I first started my work in process improvement, I would get excited along with the teams. But our Japanese counterparts would not stop there; they would be continuously looking to improve the process.

The continuous improvement process means precisely that: "it is continuous." In other words, "you cannot rest on your laurels in this system." The philosophy of Zen and "Kaizen" is reflected in the quote of Konosuke Matsushita (see "Matsushita" p. 21).

This is the foundation thinking that guides the Tribal Knowledge Paradigm. Tribal Knowledge is a continually shifting resource of a business and it needs to be guided. Ideas flow into a company and become de facto components of the Tribal Knowledge whether a manager likes it or not. So our thinking about the job of a manager is to support the improvement of Tribal Knowledge. It is a touchstone of a manager's job: Improve Tribal Knowledge in conjunction with aligning the improvement with Mission Relevance. It is our version of Kaizen: American Kaizen.

In our early days, we had a difficult time getting American workers to buy into the principles of "Kaizen." I just wasn't presenting it in quite the right way. I noticed in one company when I told the employees that I wanted them to reduce set-up from 6 hours to 1 hour, they rose to the challenge. Set-up began to go down by major improvements. And the improvements were happening very fast. But as they got to the magic number of 1 hour, the improvements started to slow.

I wanted better results and so I changed the rules. I told the production workers that I wanted to see "World Records." A world record was defined as an improvement over the previous best performance. So if the set-up was 1 hour to start, that was the world record. And if they reduced the set-up by 1 minute, that was a new record. It was an improvement. We started this process and very quickly the world record was less than 30 minutes. In the older game, I had given the employees a specific goal. When they felt that they were going to reach it, they relaxed. In this new game with the "World Record", it was now a game of "continuous improvement" or Kaizen and they loved it. But I didn't call it "Kaizen "; I called it a "World Record". And so the World Record Report evolved.

The Tribal Knowledge Council (TKC) is a part of the Kaizen process. Our goal is continuous improvement that means that we want to keep getting ideas for improvements. These ideas are submitted to the TKC, protected with No Blame and managed by the CEO and the Board. And that is how "continuous improvement" will happen.

Constantine Model of Change

One of my Organizational Development colleagues referred me to a behavioral model developed by Larry Constantine[15] as a way to describe the Quantum Leap Company "two step change process." (See Page 136, "Quantum Leap Company") The model was developed to describe Larry's work as a family therapist. In his model he makes a few observations. He noted that a family cannot move to the "Open" style of management, which is what we advocate, from the "Closed" hierarchical style (Papa's in charge) without first passing through another organization paradigm. In his words, "You have to pass through the interim step to get there."

---

[15] Constantine, Larry L. **Family Paradigms** The Guilford Press, New York, NY 1986 p 169 ff

Constantine Model of Change

Constantine

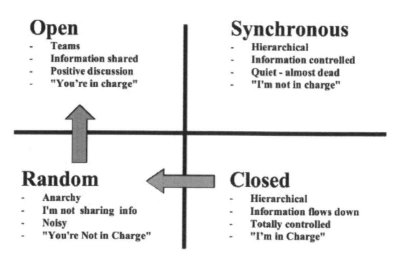

Open
- Teams
- Information shared
- Positive discussion
- "You're in charge"

Synchronous
- Hierarchical
- Information controlled
- Quiet - almost dead
- "I'm not in charge"

Random
- Anarchy
- I'm not sharing info
- Noisy
- "You're Not in Charge"

Closed
- Hierarchical
- Information flows down
- Totally controlled
- "I'm in Charge"

That is what the meta-stable state is. In the Constantine family paradigm (see diagram) if you change from a hierarchical system (as most companies are) to an open system (what the Quantum Leap Company is), you must pass through the "Random" organization.

Just a few words to expand on this and I encourage you read Constantine's Chapter 9 to see how good his model fits to the Quantum Leap. This organizational model is totally consistent with our "Quantum Leap" model.

Using this model, most of the companies that I deal with are closed organizations. They are managed from the top-down. Everyone has a defined role. Information only flows from the top and is tightly controlled. If you used one phrase to describe this organization it would be: "I'm in charge."

War on Waste Innovation

This is a dramatically different organization than the Random Organization where the operative phrase might be: "You're not in charge." As we make the change to the Open Organization, we must first pass through this Random Organization. This is analogous to the "Silicon Valley Startup" where there is really very little management. In fact, it really is organized chaos. This is a very noisy and selfish organization. Information is not readily shared. "I know how to do this and you don't," or "I know something that you don't." This is the "Metastable State" of the Quantum Leap. You don't want to be there very long but you must go through it nonetheless. I know that a company is starting to change during the War on Waste if I step out of the room. As I return and it is very noisy, this is good. In this process, noise is good. It shows that employees are feeling comfortable discussing problems. And when someone disagrees with them, they argue their case loudly as they challenge team members to support their idea.

In most of my War on Waste programs, the Metastable State will last until all the original projects of the training sessions are implemented. This might be 1 month or a year. People will feel real excited about themselves and a little more excited about the company. They begin to like coming to work again, like when the company was smaller or had just started, and they have a whole new perspective about their job.

As the company implements the TKC and new ideas begin dribbling in, there becomes a consensus that starts to build that the organization is really going to transition to the Open System that I talk about in class, the Quantum Leap Company or the Tribal Knowledge Paradigm. To the employees, it now looks like this new paradigm is a possibility. In the Open Organization, Open System or Quantum Leap Company, information is shared and there is lots of communication. In this organization, the operative words are "I'm in charge." People are empowered.

The synchronous organization would be analogous to the Utility companies where there is a totally predictable daily grind. In this organization, there is very little open discussion. Life is totally predictable. And no one wants to take charge because the operative quote that describes this organization is: "I'm not in charge." I really don't get into this type of organization at all, so I really don't have much of an opinion about what the synchronous organization is about. However, I do know about the Open, Random and Hierarchical Organizations.

It is hoped that these concepts will give us a better understanding of what happens when we change an organization. This chapter was intended to serve as a guideline in what to expect when you begin the change to the Tribal Knowledge Paradigm or theQuantum Leap Company. We know you will be excited because the end result makes our clients more profitable. And we think that is what this whole process is all about.

War on Waste Innovation

Management Tools

Our goal with WOW was to make sure that if we delivered a successful War on Waste project that it was sustainable. In order to do that, you need tools that help management guide a successful initiative after the projects are all implemented. Our approach has been successful in most of our projects but very successful in about 20% of the projects that led to the company that we call the "Tribal Knowledge Paradigm" or the "Quantum Leap Company." Hopefully all projects will be successful.

Leonard Bertain, Ph.D.

Energy Initiative

We look at any change process like War on Waste as a positive energy transfer to the company. The Second Law of Thermodynamics[i] says that open systems will tend to a state of disorder (increased entropy) if left alone. This would be like when the parents go away on a weekend and leave the 3 teenage kids alone. Without parental guidance there, the children create chaos. To counteract this reduction of order, you add energy to the household when you return. You discipline the kids and get them to clean the house. In a business analogy, you will reduce disorder and waste in your business if you add energy—and that's exactly what the War on Waste program does: it is an energy-input exercise.

Several CEOs have used this mechanism effectively to lead their companies. Jack Welch of GE and Herb Kelleher of Southwest Airlines certainly come to mind. But when I recently completed a survey of about 100 CEOs in a wide range of businesses, it became clear that this trend was definitely more than mere happenstance; it was a system that has evolved to keep companies energized. Brad Mattson of Mattson Technology, a Silicon Valley technology company, may have said it best, "Leadership is about emotion. There has to be a passion involved." And energy initiatives are activities to stir the emotions. People stay excited when energy is pouring into the company. Over the years, we have noticed that this energy mechanism takes a few different forms:

The Big Deal: In the Big Deal, a big jolt of energy is infused into the company using a big initiative that produces enough energy for the company to feed off for the next three or four years. GE did this with great success. In fact, it was Jack Welch's great success here that energized GE over a 20-year period with 5 major initiatives.

140

War on Waste Innovation

The Wing Ding: Smaller, more frequent, "zany" initiatives produce a consistent level of energy. Southwest Airline's Herb Kelleher produces a Wing Ding about every four to six months and keeps everyone energized.

The Technology Hype: The volatility of the high-tech industry provides its own on-going, intoxicating energy hype. Brad Mattson, CEO and founder of Mattson Technology, noted that this continual production of energy keeps technology workers on their toes, ready to act with a sense of urgency.

The Fan Club Industry: Some companies hire employees who are intensely infatuated with their technology, products or services, which creates a tremendous source of energy within the company. Ray Dolby of Dolby Laboratories hires employees who are almost all audiophiles; they love the product offered by Dolby Laboratories and use it at home every day. They are true fans of the company's products.

Customer Retention Initiative – A number of CEO's noted that their most successful initiatives were those focused on customers. Once employees understand the value of retaining a customer, then a tremendous amount of energy is generated by the "customer retention" initiatives. Jan Carlzon of SAS Airlines created just such an initiative with the "Moments of Truth" concept. In fact, his effort in this regard was so successful that the Moments of Truth ideas became ingrained into the culture of the company during his reign.

Of course, there may be a good deal more methods to achieve this energy infusion process. Understanding how a company manages the infusion of energy is very important. We are so convinced of the power of the Energy Initiative that we define it to be one of the 6 job responsibilities of the CEO: "Understand how you add energy to the company and then

141

Leonard Bertain, Ph.D.

look for the next Energy Initiative if your business requires one."

Originally, we thought that you should have an ongoing series of energy initiatives to make our concept work. But as we evolved our thinking, we realized that ideally you use the energy initiative to kick-start the process. And then the Tribal Knowledge Paradigm takes over and continues to keep the energy up by supporting the on-going flow of ideas into the company. It becomes all managers' responsibility to lead with this guideline of action: improve Tribal Knowledge in alignment with the Mission of the company. It is what we call American Kaizen.

Pioneers and Settlers

This is not a complicated concept. It goes like this.

There are some people who are pioneers and some who are settlers. I like to think that the whole human population breaks down into this binary division. We need both. And we can't all be pioneers. In fact, we like the idea that there is some distribution of people into the two categories. And here is why.

The pioneers are the people with the wild ideas. They are the ones who push the limits of managers. In the Wild, Wild West, they were the guys who dared to go where no man had gone before. They set up the new territories and the settlers made the lands livable. There would have been neither development without the pioneers nor stability without the settlers.

The Pioneer is the entrepreneur who ventures out into the unknown. He is the adventurer who is looking for new territory, the entrepreneur making new markets. The Pioneer is

142

War on Waste Innovation

the first to volunteer for the highly risky new assignment and the pioneer is very difficult to manage.

The Settler goes in after the pioneer and makes things work. The Settler stabilizes the rules of the business. The Settler is "steady as she goes." But no organization can run with just Pioneers or Settlers. The ideas of how to deal with these two diverse characters are part of leading the Quantum Leap Company.

I remember one incident a number of years ago. A CEO had noticed that one of his teams was not working as well as another one. When I asked him to tell me what the makeup of pioneers and settlers was, he almost started laughing. As soon as I asked the question, he knew what was coming next. In his situation, he had put 5 pioneers on the unsuccessful team. After I asked the question, he immediately knew what to do. He replaced two of the pioneers with settlers and the team then was able to function. So the message here is don't put teams together with all pioneers or all settlers. Mix them up.

When it comes to determining whether a particular person is a pioneer or settler, I don't get very fancy. I don't have any particular test; I just use my "gut" to guide me. In fact, when making assessments of people, don't worry that you might make a mistake in your assessment. There is nothing good or bad about either behavior. The classification is just a useful assessment tool to try to understand your management team and employees.

An interesting situation occurred at one company where I had explained the concept of Pioneers and Settlers to the management team. One of the executives who I had identified as a settler, really wanted to be pegged as a pioneer. He was obsessed with being a pioneer. He was the Vice President of Sales and was a very successful salesman. There is an expectation that you have to be a pioneer to be a good salesman. But that isn't necessarily so. This guy was an excellent salesman. In his industry, a good settler was able to sell to the customers because they liked his laid back style. He had a good sense of humor that was very subtle. But he was a settler. There was nothing I could do about that. He had to live with it. Eventually, he did.

Simplification as a Strategy

> "Anyone can make the simple complicated, creativity is making the complicated simple." *Charlie Mingus*

Strategy was discussed earlier. It means more that articulating strategies in such a way that they are clear, concise and simple. What it really means is that simplification makes all processes efficient. It makes instructions to employees precise and understandable. It forces managers to define clear measurements of performance. All thinking in the company is geared to "KISS" (keep it simple stupid). All this simplification creates an organization that is geared for action. Everyone knows what to do. And when people fail to do their jobs, others let them know. It's OK to do that in a "No Blame" work environment.

And the reason that simplification becomes a "strategy" is that it now becomes possible to make the statement: "We will make money for our shareholders by running the business with simple, clear procedures that everyone can understand. And by doing so, we'll maximize the revenues and optimize the profits for those revenues."

As an example, one of my friends, Jim Horan, has developed a program he calls "the one-page business plan." He has written a book of the same title. As you might expect, this book describes a very simple process of creating a business

144

plan. It is 100 pages or so. Jim has done a good job of explaining to the novice how a one-page business plan is created. But it is not easy. There is some significant thinking that goes into such a process. But the "one page business plan" is part of the simplification process that is discussed here. If your thinking can be compressed to one page, you have done a marvelous job of simplification.

The simplification process applies to all aspects of the business: how we get products to market, how we market, how we sell, how we engineer. Everything that is written for any process needs to be said with the fewest and most concise choice of words. By so doing, simplification becomes ingrained in the company.

Sense of Urgency

Everyone loves Tom Cruise's line in "Top Gun," and he delivers it with such gusto, "I have a need for speed." A company with a Sense of Urgency is just like that, "it has a need for speed." In the "urgency company" – the company with a sense of urgency – everyone understands that the urgency condition can be activated at any moment. In this company, when the urgency switch is turned on, the "urgency condition" is activated and everyone understands what to do.

One of the goals that I give every company is to design your production capacity to function on a daily basis at 80% of peak capacity. Then when you need that extra 20% you turn on the urgency switch.

We distinguish "urgency" from "chaos" in this context. We don't like chaos. We like urgency. The chaotic organization is always in the fire-fighting mode. There is no planning, or if there is, there is very little planning. Every order is hot. Customers know that to get their orders acted on they need to talk to the President. However, in the company that can effectively respond to the "urgency condition", everything is in order. It's just that when the urgency condition is activated, everyone knows what to do. For instance, when a new large "elephant" order from an old client comes in the door, the activity levels are just stepped up a bit. These conditions activate the "urgency switch".

Urgency Switch

In the company that can respond to urgent conditions in a systematic way, they know when the Urgency Switch is on. I like to say that the Urgency Switch is not a variable control switch that is somewhere between off and full speed ahead. When the Urgency Switch is on everyone knows it and it is "damn the torpedoes full speed ahead." The difference between the chaotic organization and the urgency organization is that in the urgency organization when the urgency switch is on, the company is moving at a faster pace. All systems are capable of going a notch faster than normal but this urgency condition does not radically change the way things are done. In other words, the normal speed of operation is a pacing speed that can be turned up to respond to an urgent condition.

I learned all about one of those companies when I worked for my Dad. On Monday morning, he turned the urgency switch on. He left it on all week and on Saturday, about 5:15 PM, he was ready to turn it off. He loved to work that way and for the most part he survived doing that for a long time. He lived to be a very old man. So the chaos condition is not necessarily bad for the person who turns the switch on. It is bad for the participants doing their jobs. I know all about it. Working in that environment grated on my nerves and I didn't like it. I have never liked working like that. When I see it in a company that I work with, I go to work and try to fix that problem quickly.

Work

We define work and jobs as having three elements (PCD):

- **Planning** the work,

- **Controlling** it (which includes measuring and adjusting the work when the results aren't quite right)

- **Doing** the work.

In the usual scheme of things, for most work processes, the managers do the planning and controlling. Of course, workers perform the "doing" part of work. When true empowerment is desired for the work team, the planning and control functions associated with the work of the team need to be handled by the team. So, to empower the team, the manager must relinquish these planning and control work functions. Most managers and supervisors resist this loss of power, fearing that nothing will replace it. As we see it, fear of the loss of power and control is usually at the heart of management's resistance to change.

Obviously, there can be managerial concern about the "yes/no" Charts or any part of the process that is out of the manager's control. If some of the control (measuring and then adjusting) is now in the hands of the work team, then there is less need for supervision to make decisions about the work. Then what does a supervisor or manager do with the time previously spent controlling the work (and the workers)? This is a realistic concern, but if the manager is truly concerned about work performance, what difference does it make in how it is accomplished? Now the supervisor or manager can devote time to another high priority issue. When our clients find this is an issue, we routinely see that they redirect supervisory personnel to such activities as coaching, facilitating, teaching, expediting, project work, etc.

This is the basic management required in the Tribal Knowledge Paradigm. Managers need to help all employees improve Tribal Knowledge that is aligned with company mission. All of these activities are performed as a service to the value-adding activities carried out by their supervisees.

Creating the Quantum Leap Company

As we have created over 20 Quantum Leap companies, we have observed the following characteristics of each.

Step 1: Lead the War on Waste Program. The CEO agrees to participate, lead the War on Waste Program and follow the procedures of change defined during the War on Waste. The CEO leads this change initiative, the Phase 0 initiative, and does not pass the responsibility to others. Certainly others may be commissioned to help but the responsibility falls directly on the CEO.

Step 2: Improve Tribal Knowledge. If you get nothing else from this encyclopedia, understand this: recognizing the importance of ideas is crucial to the success of this paradigm. The War on Waste protects the idea from renegade managers and other naysayers. If ideas have an opportunity to thrive, profits will follow. In a way, this is the magic of this process.

Step 3: Manage Innovation. In order to ensure a continuous flow of ideas, the CEO must agree to implement a system of Innovation Management to make sure that process improvement and new business ideas are encouraged. The War on Waste establishes the TKC (Tribal Knowledge Council), described elsewhere in this encyclopedia. The TKC will be responsible for supporting innovation ideas for new market or business opportunities.

Step 4: Manage Change. The CEO must agree that he or she will be in charge of change management within the company. It is not the job of a Change Agent—the CEO manages the Change Agent, not the other way around. The CEO must also be alert for the Blue Bird or the Killer App that surfaces as the Tribal Knowledge Council reviews ideas for action. This is a learned skill and CEOs needs to open their eyes for these ideas at the source.

Step 5: Define the Energy Initiative Plan for the Company. As noted under Energy Initiative, the key to a sustained corporate energy level is implementing a program to ensure an on-going infusion of energy into the company. This is done with one initial energy infusion and is sustained by support of Tribal Knowledge improvement actions from all managers.

Quantum Nudge

In the diagram below, the Quantum Nudge is the energy input required to move the company from the metastable first level to the Second Excited State. A company receives a good dose of energy as a result of the War on Waste Program.

Leonard Bertain, Ph.D.

The Quantum Leap

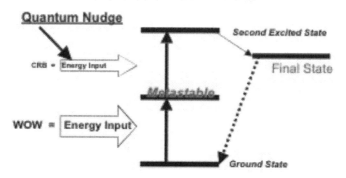

Company

So if an event occurs and a company gets enough energy to make it to the Second Excited State, it will have made the Quantum Leap. We call this energy input, the "Quantum Nudge" because to get the results of the Quantum Leap, you don't have to put much energy into the company. After the War on Waste, the company is poised to make the Quantum Leap. You just have to nudge it to get the desired result. If you read the book, "The Tribal Knowledge Paradox – Using WOW to align Strategy with Process," by the author, you will understand how hard it is to complete a War on Waste. It requires a good deal of energy and that is noted on the chart as the WOW – Energy Input.

The Scientific Paradigm

My background in science has allowed me to look at business through the lens of "science." In many ways that has been good for my clients because they looked to me to help them understand what was going on during the War on Waste projects. The following terms and my use of them in describing what was going on in the War on Waste have evolved from these "science insights." The term "paradigm" comes up as a way to describe these new rules of managing a business. With a scientific spin these rules just might help you.

Leonard Bertain, Ph.D.

Scientific Paradigm

A paradigm is a set of rules. The scientific paradigm then would be the set of rules that guide the scientist. This is the scientific method. The resulting organization run by the rules of the scientific method would be the Scientific Paradigm.

The process begins with a scientific attitude (No Blame). It was clear that in order to affect change in business it must be done from a perspective of "change without reprisal." In other words, people needed to be free to input ideas for change without fear of reprisal from a boss or a management system or style of management that resists new ideas. In order to change, new ideas are needed. So we established a philosophy of "No Blame." We don't care who or what is responsible for the problem, we just want to identify a problem and then fix it with a cost-effective solution.

When you draw a parallel to Science, you find that the scientific inquiry is exactly the same. In Science, we don't care why our theory can't explain a particular phenomenon; we want to know how we can explain it. In Science, we never look for the idiot who developed a particular theory to explain a phenomenon and then blame him or her for the problems that theory presents. We collect data in Science and then try to fit the data to a theory, which can explain it. All of this is carried out in an atmosphere of "No Blame."

The War on Waste is an approach to business improvement that uses all of the power of the scientific approach to problem identification and problem solving. It uses both linear thinking and non-linear thinking. But more than anything, it really turns a company into a learning organization, into a company that respects ideas for being introduced in the first place, their originality and their implementation.

152

War on Waste Innovation

In the formal training program, we teach students to ask precise, unambiguous, and incisive questions about important business issues, by using a very precise but flexible interrogation methodology. The approach teaches a directed probing technique that is protected from the resistance to change by the umbrella of the "No Blame" Philosophy.

The Scientific Paradigm helps us investigate problems with great clarity. It provides a powerful, methodology to predict, investigate and explain. And it teaches us to analyze exactly and by applying that analysis we can see what is coming down the road a bit. The War on Waste is the particular investigation approach we use as the first step of our journey.

Energy

I was trained as a Physicist and consider analogies from Physics to be perfectly acceptable in describing business systems. Energy is a powerful concept of physics. It provides us with a way to quantify the forces of nature by the actions that they produce. Energy exists in a gravitational field by the forces that attract material bodies to each other because of their distances from each other. When I hold a ball above my head and drop it, I convert the potential energy that it had when it rested in my hand to kinetic energy that it has because it is moving to the ground. It has velocity. And the velocity increases because of the acceleration given to the falling body by the force of gravity. The force of gravity (a force) creates both "potential" and "kinetic" energy.

Likewise, electrons and protons have energies because there is an electromagnetic force of interaction between the two particles. A similar concept applies to nuclear particles, protons and neutrons. In this case, the force is called a "nuclear force." And the energy that is tied up in the nuclear interaction is called "nuclear energy". The release of the

Leonard Bertain, Ph.D.

energy that binds nuclear particles is what causes thermonuclear explosions.

So how do we convert these concepts to business? Basically, we have evolved terms like "forcing function" to describe a business activity that causes some significant business result. It is the force that causes the result.

For instance, a new product is a "forcing function" that will cause new orders to roll in. A marketing campaign on television can be a "forcing function" to bring attention and orders to a new product offering. And somehow, these forcing functions cause significantly "energized" businesses.

We talk about needing "a company with a sense of urgency". The sense of urgency implies that the company is prepared for action. It has the potential to act given the right situation. And when that situation occurs everyone in the company knows that prompt attention is required to deal with the opportunity. So we say that the company is "energized." It has lots of energy. It has gone from the "potential" energy state waiting for action to the "kinetic energy" state when it is reacting to an urgent condition.

I have asked a number of CEO's what they wanted from their organizations. All of them said that they wanted "high energy" companies that responded to customer's requirements effectively on a daily basis. When the situation required it, it went into overdrive. Not organized chaos, but overdrive. The company with "a sense of urgency" is one with a propensity for action. Customers like doing business with this company because of its urgency of activity. It has a commitment to get things done.

To be more systematic about this, think of all the actions that happen in business as being results of a business force.

154

War on Waste Innovation

When everyone is energized, I look for the force. What is causing all this energy? In fact, velocity is one physics concept that has been used to describe business. One definition links speed to the ratio of cycle time and lead-time. If products move through a business fast, then inventory stays for shorter periods, less inventory is required (reduced costs – direct to the bottom line) and money comes in faster.

A sidebar on the subject of energy is one that I have been thinking about a long time. How do you measure "business energy?" We have lots of measures to tell us about how a company is performing but none of them are uniquely capable of telling us how much energy a company has. I once wrote an article about this. When I showed this article to a CEO a number of years ago, he said that he couldn't imagine this would be a very useful concept for his organization because he was having a hard time getting his people to read an income statement and understand it. How can you possibly help me with this kind of crap?

I don't consider it intellectual crap but I do understand that it stretches one's thinking to imagine a powerful new way to measure a CEO. I liked the results of the analysis because it made sense. But we really don't need another CEO measure. We just need to be extremely good at paying attention to the measures that we currently have.

One of the critical activities a CEO can undertake is to find new ways of inputting energy into the company. Jack Welch used energy to crank up GE every four years or so with one of his initiatives. Herb Kelleher of Southwest Airlines does the same thing more frequently with less comprehensive programs. Energy is necessary to ensure that the company stays organized and far away from the edge of chaos.

Leonard Bertain, Ph.D.

Entropy

Entropy is an odd term in physics that is used to measure the order or disorder of a physical system. The most common application of the term is in conjunction with Energy as defined in the Second Law of Thermodynamics. This law is known as the "Conservation of Energy" which says that open systems will tend to a state of disorder (increased entropy) if left alone (decreased energy). If energy increases, entropy decreases and vice versa. You might be able to understand it like this. You go away on a vacation and the kids mess up the house. Without your energy there, they return to chaos. To counteract this reduction of order, you add energy to the system when you return; you discipline the kids and clean the house.

In a business analogy, the War on Waste (WOW) is an energy infusion initiative. WOW increases energy and reduces the disorder of your business.

Any of the following programs that get the employees excited about their jobs are energy initiatives: Quality Circles, Re-engineering, TQM, 6-Sigma and the War on Waste Programs. These programs add energy to the organization and therefore reduce entropy. On the flip side, we find that management's lack of attention to an organization will lead to lost energy that equates to increased entropy and therefore increased disorder. We see this all the time. Many CEOs think that once they get their business organized and profitable then they could relax, sit back and enjoy the profits. It doesn't work that way. As a CEO you have to keep pouring energy into the company to keep it from falling into the chaos of disorder. In fact, it is one of our defined responsibilities of a CEO that s/he is on the lookout for the next source of energy infusion for the company.

War on Waste Innovation

Non-linear thinking

Traditional school programs teach us using linear methodologies. Linear thinking teaches us that every problem (the manifestation of an effect) has a cause. With linear thinking we are taught how to link a cause to an effect. It teaches that for each problem there is a "right solution". Further, it teaches that there is a right way to solve a problem. And the solution techniques are based on Aristotelian logic that has permeated Western thinking since the Middle Ages.

For example, accounting is a linear thinking discipline - capture data on a general ledger account, roll the numbers up to a summary account and make a decision based on the output. If the number is high, we do X, if it is right on we do nothing, and if it is low we do Y. Nice and ducky! Finance tells us what investment to make based on numbers. Economics and finance tells us to open a new plant in Texas based on forecasts of economic indicators of a rapid growth in a particular segment of the market for the South Central section of the US. The logic is irrefutable, determine the cause of an effect and the action is very clear.

Linear thinking demands results. Linear thinkers have to blame someone to move forward. "If someone isn't to blame, we wouldn't have a problem here." "Someone has definitely screwed up and we need to find that person."

Unfortunately business decisions are largely non-linear. They flow from intuition and not logic. They are jumps of thought and are probably more emotionally based than rationally based. Non-linear thinking says that there is more than one solution to any problem. Non-linear thinking says that there is no right way to solve a business problem.

Leonard Bertain, Ph.D.

In fact, I use the example of solving an equation in algebra to make an analogy here. If you are given 10 equations and 10 unknowns, you can solve the equations exactly following the linear thinking model of Algebra. But when you have 10 equations and 20 unknowns, many solutions will fit the equations. And that is what non-linear thinkers have to do. They choose one of the many solutions to those equations and run with it. Experience, intuition, logic, common sense, whatever you can muster is used to make the decision.

I like to tell clients that it doesn't make sense to worry about whether you have the right solution because tomorrow's problem was today's solution. In other words, you make a decision today based on all the facts that you have at your fingertips and you run with the solution. Don't look back because you can be guaranteed that it is going to be a problem. "Today's solution is tomorrow's problem."

I remember one day after I had labored for 11 hours in front of employees at a metal cutting manufacturing plant that made a valve used in the semi-conductor industry. I was tired. I really wanted to go home. The employees at this particular company were feisty and required a lot of my energy. One of the employees who had ended his shift about an hour before had stayed around to talk to me. By the way, that is not unusual because when you begin a War on Waste engagement, people take it very seriously and are willing to put in an extra effort to make it succeed. He told me that he had been thinking about what I was saying in class and he had stayed around to discuss with me his violent disagreement with me on one thing.

As he told me his problem, I was suddenly hit with an inspiration. This man had objected to my statement that the program that I was delivering was "logical." He told me "it wasn't logical at all. But it made sense." After he said that, I

158

was flummoxed for a moment. But he was right. What I was saying in class was not rigorously true in pure "Aristotelian logic." But it made business sense. The machinist was worrying about the lack of preciseness to the War on Waste process. It does not generate precise solutions. It gives employees who are implementing solutions lots of "wiggle room" in their implementation. We say in the War on Waste, "that's OK if it doesn't work, find out why it didn't work, test another solution and move on." Just do it. But it works because it moves the company forward. It causes productivity to improve and people involved in the process feel engaged in the business.

Non-linear thinking says that it is better to do something than nothing. Action is more important than the immediate results. Non-linear thinking says that progress is made when an action takes place. We learn from our efforts and anything is better than nothing. We usually don't do things to commit suicide in business. But we know that we will make mistakes. If it doesn't work that's OK because we have just learned another way that didn't work.

The War on Waste is rooted in non-linear logic. We don't need to blame someone to move forward. It doesn't make sense to blame someone for a problem. Just fix it. This is all part of creating a company with a sense of urgency. Make a decision, learn from it and then improve it.

More of management decision-making is based on non-linear thinking than we realize. For instance, "I don't care what you do, just do something." Urgency management is a non-linear process. It is based on 5/67 action (5% of the features give 67% of the benefit), not rigorous logic. "Just get going." "Forget all the procedures, forget the crap about why things aren't getting done and just get going." "We need to get

Leonard Bertain, Ph.D.

some output (results) out of this plant." "But we have to make sure that all the waste is totally eliminated."

The reason that the War on Waste works so well is that it has a singular focus. Eliminate this waste by following the Scientific Method. The process begins by collecting data that quantifies the size of the waste. The "linear thinking" approach to this is to collect a bunch of data, and you can't do any analysis until you have a lot of it (statistically significant samples). And then you analyze the detail out of the data and it confuses the people that need to use the information. The "non-linear" approach would begin by collecting data for a few days (a little data - spot check and see what that tells you). This is where we discovered the value "5/67 Thinking." We looked at only 5% of the total data and we made a decision that was pretty solid when we looked back on the results.

I love to do this with the "anal-retentive" linear thinkers because it blows their minds. They can't make a decision unless there is tons of data to substantiate a point.

Let me give you a good example. A client of mine made DNA Oligos. They are the small segments of DNA used by biotech researchers to probe the inner workings of DNA and organisms. They were having a problem trying to get to the root cause of a particular problem. The team working on this problem was stymied. I told them to get off their butts and get me some information. Then one of the guys stepped up and said, "Oh, I get it. We aren't doing basic research here are we? We are doing "practical" research." I laughed and sent them on their way. I wanted them to analyze one week of data that they already had in the files. I wanted them to tell me how many problem oligos they had, how they broke down by type. After they did that we looked at their data. Now, they didn't have "statistically significant" volumes of data. But they had

160

analyzed over 1 week of data and had 600 bad "parts." They deduced where they should spend their time to fix the problem.

The focus was on the process of one of the departments. I asked the CEO to give me his assessment of the problem before they started. He told me that his hunch was going to be that same department. And the fun thing about this process was that it only took the team of 5 people to analyze the data and come back with numbers in two hours that confirmed his guess.

My point here is that the Scientific Paradigm has its roots in non-linear thinking. But the focus on Waste elimination keeps the team's problem solving on track. Eliminate the waste by collecting enough data to convince any decision making doubters that there is a problem and then you can go forward with your solution. If every decision in business followed this methodology, fewer catastrophic decisions would be made.

Many CEO's make decisions thinking that they have "statistically significant" numbers to back up their decision. My point is that when all is said and done, most CEO's don't need a lot of data and information to guide their decision-making, they just need a little information and they will be right most of the time.

This is more of the rationale as to why the 5/67 Rule works. I had an early business mentor that told me that if 50% of his decisions turned out to be right, he was a genius. He felt that, as CEO, if he was close to 50% right in his decisions, he should keep his job.

Scientific Attitude

When you draw a parallel to Science, you find that the scientific inquiry is exactly the same. In Science, we don't

Leonard Bertain, Ph.D.

care why our theory can't explain a particular phenomenon; we want to know how we can explain it. In Science, we never look for the idiot who developed a particular theory to explain a phenomenon and then blame him or her for the problems that a theory presents. We collect data in Science and then try to fit the data to a theory, which can explain it. All of this is carried out in an atmosphere of "No Blame."

It is clear that in order to affect change in business it must be done from a perspective of "change without reprisal." In other words, people needed to be free to input ideas for change without fear of reprisal from a boss or a management system or style of management that resists new ideas. In order to change, new ideas are needed. So we established a philosophy of "No Blame." We don't care who or what is responsible for the problem, we just want to identify a problem and then fix it with a cost-effective solution.

Uncertainty principle

The uncertainty principle rocked the world of Physics in 1927 when Werner Heisenberg concluded that the rules of measurement of the macro world did not apply to the micro world. He perplexed his fellow scientists with this startling revelation because his theory established a de-coupling of key micro indicators (location and momentum) in a way never imagined. The essence of the Uncertainty Principle is that as you study the atom and the fundamental particles of matter, you will have problems trying to get all the information with the precision that you need. You may know exactly where an electron is in space but you won't know anything about its momentum (like how fast it was moving). And vice versa. Who could have imagined that our ways of measuring things in our visual world did not apply to the micro world?

War on Waste Innovation

A number of years ago, I was struck by a "Heisenberg Uncertainty" condition when I was trying to get a company to deliver both quality and high productivity at the same time. One of the workers said, "Your can have our product fast, cheap or better. Pick two." He was giving me back the company line that a type of "Uncertainty Principle" was at work in American business.

I have never bought that line. You can do all three and that is what we try to do in the War on Waste. If you can increase productivity with dramatic worker productivity (no matter what the business), you should be able to do so with both high quality and a sense of urgency. And we have done this time and again. There is no "Uncertainty Condition" at work, only laziness.

A corollary effect of the Uncertainty Principle in business is a principle known as the Hawthorne effect. One way to summarize the Hawthorne effect, "if you watch a worker and you have a stop watch in your hand for him to see, you will get different results than if you do the same test while out of sight of the worker." In other words, your presence alters the measurements. The worker feels that big brother is watching if you stand out in the work area with the stopwatch. In other words, you can interfere with productivity measurements when you measure them.

That is also a corollary of the "Uncertainty Principle." If you try to get all the information that you can about the position of the electron, you will have little information about the momentum. In other words, the precise measurement of electron position almost destroys all information that we have about momentum. So when I walk out on to a factory floor with my stopwatch and workers see it, they change their production rates and my measurements lose their accuracy. In

163

Leonard Bertain, Ph.D.

other words, the workers change their normal work rate when they see managers measuring them.

So our solution is to let the people do their own measurement and then hold them to high performance standards with continuous improvement measurements using the "World Record Report" (See "World Record Report") or similar measurement tool. And this way, we get accurate, reliable information.

War on Waste Innovation

War on Waste Consequences

The following observations have helped me understand what happens when we deliver a War on Waste. We have focused our efforts at trying to understand how the Quantum Leap Company evolves. We also need to know what we have to do to make it happen. The Quantum Leap Company or its attendant management structure, the Tribal Knowledge Paradigm, is our term to describe the company that has made a major, positive change in its profit structure. We want to tell people about what makes this happen and hope others will do the same for us. It is important to understand this company.

Leonard Bertain, Ph.D.

Quantum Leap Company

Early on we struggled to define what this company was all about. We had observed that some companies made a leap in improvement during or immediately following the War on Waste. It was a significant leap in performance improvement. "Why did it occur?" was certainly a good question to ask. We'll explore that later. But what are the characteristics of this company? We wanted to know how we would recognize when the Quantum Leap had occurred? Or better yet, can we do anything to make it happen?

First, we made a few observations about the Quantum Leap companies. We noted that the presentations during the War on Waste created a major excitement in the company. Employees became energized and began to feel a greater sense of pride in their work. Employees told us that War on Waste projects gave them a real sense of empowerment. They were energized to do more. This is the first step of the Quantum Leap (see Diagram). All companies that we have worked with usually get this far. But it is a mandatory first step, the first step of the Quantum Leap.

War on Waste Innovation

The Quantum Leap

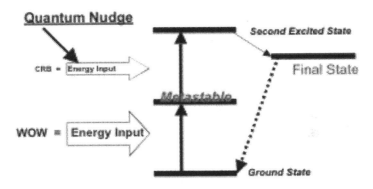

Company

After a company makes this first step, it could remain there for days, months or years. We call this step a meta-stable state because the company can improve or return to where it was before the training began. It is in a fragile state. A Black Knight (see "Black Knight") that went through the War on Waste training or a Black Knight who is new to the company and not familiar with the Quantum Leap Company culture can destroy the company at this point. The Black Knight can create doubt in the commitment of the CEO to the success of the War on Waste. It is at this point that we encourage CEO's to explain to everyone the consequences of failing to get behind his agenda.

The second step of the War on Waste will make the company a lot of money in improved profits and so traitors are not welcome. To make this second step of the Quantum Leap, the company is poised for action as a result of the initial activity from the War on Waste. The "Quantum Nudge" will move the company to the Second Excited State. This nudge

167

may come at any time. And it takes lots of forms.

For example, in one company the Quantum Nudge came when an employee approached me to ask help in keeping the CEO out of his way so that he could develop a special robotic controlled version of the traditional chemical process of the company. He needed someone to keep the meddling CEO and founder from interfering with his new design. It turned out to be a Quantum Leap because the company was able to capture significant new business at lower and more profitable levels than with the older process. This led to the company growing 3 times its previous year's revenues. It ultimately led to a sale of the company at over 12 times EBITDA 10 months after the War on Waste.

In another Quantum Leap company, the Quantum Nudge idea came from one of the employees after the presentations were complete. The employee observed that once they had organized templates that had been badly disorganized, they could respond to any product request and have it completed in less than an hour. That meant that the company could now serve a market in which customers needed "May Day" service. The company could charge a premium to get the product to the customer because the customer's equipment was down. The company could "same day" ship products to the East Coast from California if the order was received by 4:00 PM. This idea allowed the company to become the prime supplier of product to this market. And the Quantum Leap was achieved.

Another Quantum Leap company completed the War on Waste and had improved its operating processes. The Quantum Leap came several months later when they found that they could deliver a sample product with each quote to their largest customer. They ended up getting all of the customer's business because the customer felt more comfortable giving them the business. This company grew for three years with a 25% pre-tax profit. They were sold 4 years after the War on Waste for 13 times EBITDA.

Many of these Quantum Leaps occurred with our facilitators on site. Some of them occurred when we had completed our consulting assignment. In just about all of these situations, the CEO realized that the War on Waste prepared the way for the Quantum Leap idea. The idea emerges and the company can be guided easily to make the idea happen. The precise nature of any company's Quantum Leap is not predictable. But if an idea leads to a 30% improvement in profit, lead-time, or direct labor productivity after the War on Waste, then a Quantum Leap has probably occurred. These are just some of the indicators but if the Quantum Leap has occurred, significant improvement will be noted in most key business indicators. We generally are looking to see Gross Margin Improvements of 20% or greater, revenue increases from the Quantum Leap idea of at least 50% and lead time reductions of at least 50%.

Speed (Velocity)

When we talk about Speed or Velocity of a business we are referring to the rate at which it delivers the value-adding process to its customers. And we know that competitors with the shortest product development, manufacturing and distribution cycles will dominate their markets. We know this because they have the advantage of optimized processes, innovation, flexibility, and low cost.

The War on Waste is all about increasing the velocity of the change process. The Winners of today's market competitions are going to be those companies that figure out ways to get their products to market quickest. Additionally, in order to thrive, an organization must be able to transform itself and its underlying business strategy quickly and efficiently.

The company that competes aggressively in today's market will look for opportunities for earnings growth. In the War on Waste, we look for opportunities to resolve critical constraints by:

- Shortening cycle times,

- Speeding cash flow,

- Eliminating wasteful non-value-adding costs,

- Reducing the need for working capital,

- Reducing warrantees and improving service.

We have done a lot of work with companies in helping them increase the operating speeds of processes. We improved a company's lead-time on one project from 22 days to 2 days. That is, the lead-time measured from receipt of the order until the product was shipped. In this company, all orders were shipped to the customers on a COD basis so the lead-time we decided to measure was the time from receipt of the order until the product was paid for. The cycle time went from 1 day to 4 hours. After this War on Waste activity, the company was really buzzing. Things started to happen.

We believe that by focusing your organization on increasing the throughput of your organization (its speed) you are going to totally change the way you do business. And the control you had before may not be the control that you ultimately want to have. Rest assured, your organization is going to change. If you get your employees to focus on speed, you will suddenly find that they will be begin to do the right work in order to increase the speed.

When delivery times go down, customers are happier, more customers want the benefit of your fast delivery, and your business or organization prospers. This leads to a company with a sense of urgency.

A happy coincidence of bringing more customers to your door is that you now have the option of raising your prices. If customers recognize that your fast delivery time offers a benefit not to be found with your competitors, they will pay a bit more for the added value your fast delivery time provides. So, you can now earn more for the same work, allowing you to take bigger profits and share some with the employees, thus increasing their commitment to improving delivery still more.

Customer Centric

This means putting the customer at the center of your business. It means defining your relationship so that your customer understands that it is a smart thing to do business with you. The term "customer centric" evolved from the "new economy" world in which the Internet began to interact with companies and their relationships with their customers in a new way. The Internet made it easier for companies to switch from one supplier to the next. This meant that survival was dependent on a business 101 maxim, "pay attention to your customers, after all they help pay your bills."

This meant that a company had better figure out how to service customers. Because many companies were terrible in doing this, moving to a "customer centric" focus meant fixing the business holistically. It meant re-engineering the company to insure success. It is not possible to give lip service to a "customer centric" demand from the market. The New

Leonard Bertain, Ph.D.

Economy focus is being tuned in to the customer to the extent that the customer is seen as a partner.

The War on Waste in conjunction with the Moment of Truth analysis is a thorough way to examine the degree to which a company is focused on serving its customers. The degree that you are **not** focused on the customer will appear as a waste during the War on Waste process.

I used to hate going to shop at Safeway Stores. Now I love it. Although Safeway stores did not use a War on Waste process, they used a similar concept of analysis and they invested heavily in training their employees to think about the impact on profits of providing better customer service. Now, when I walk in the door, the employees actually smile at me. I am their customer. If I don't know where the bread is, they will show me or if I need more help, they will walk me over to the bread shelf and then ask if I need any more help. All I can say is, the Safeway employees now understand the idea of serving customers. And it works for me. This way of doing business is clearly customer centric. You never hear a Safeway employee bitching about you interrupting them with a question. It's wonderful and it's profitable because it's gotten my business back.

Edge of chaos

Complex systems (like businesses) strike a balance between the need for order and the imperative to change. The edge of chaos is the place where there is enough innovation to keep a living system vibrant and enough stability to keep it from collapsing into anarchy. Only on the edge of chaos can complex systems flourish. As a CEO moves forward in today's economy, there is no guarantee of success. The path forward is walking on the edge of chaos. And there are no maps.

War on Waste Innovation

As an example of this, a recent client had wonderful results from the War on Waste. The company had not made a Quantum Leap yet but it was showing dramatic improvement in the productivity measures of employees. Then the CEO made an interesting move. He hired a guy who had not been through the War on Waste. He had not worked with War on Waste before. In the interview process, this guy had all the right rhetoric. He talked about War on Waste concepts after reading some of the background materials. He talked positively about teams, measures and employee recognition, the whole story that we preach. But when he came on board, "tension developed." The company culture was used to dealing with the CEO and there was a bit of a rebellion on the staff when the new guy tried to implement some change. Chaos ensued. And it had only taken 4 months. The company had slipped into the abyss of chaos.

What should the CEO do? His company was now in trouble. He had the innovation machine working fine with the TKC (Tribal Knowledge Council). Ideas were flourishing. The employees were comfortable with their production process that had been dramatically improved from the War on Waste. Employee output as measured in revenues per value-added hour worked increased 3-fold. The Quantum Leap had not been achieved but ideas were being floated around to achieve the Quantum Leap. The War on Waste led to a re-examination of what customers were going to be pursued. It was determined that the company needed to redefine itself. It needed a new culture. The CEO had evolved the culture of his current company over 20 years and his behavior and management character had changed over that time. He needed a culture that reflected the company that he wanted to manage in the future and that had the values and the ethos that he believed. The new manager wasn't totally wrong but his ideas were not flowing easily into the company.

So the CEO did what he did best. He acted immediately to address the company's culture. He had paid attention to a yellow card that I had given him. On it I had included the 6 things that I think every CEO should do. They are:

1. Manage Strategy,

2. Improve Tribal Knowledge.

3. Manage Innovation,

4. Oversee key hires,

5. Develop and manager the company culture,

6. Manage change,

The CEO had done a good job of managing change through the War on Waste. He had made a hire that was difficult but he was going to make that work. He was doing a good job of innovation and he was capturing the energy infusion started with the War on Waste initiative. Where he needed help was in the culture development and the strategy development.

We worked on the culture first. We spent a few days analyzing the strengths and weaknesses of his current culture with the CEO and his key managers. We worked on defining the new culture and we got input from all the key sales, engineering and production managers. In one of the off-site sessions, we spent a night at a J. W. Marriott Hotel.

The staff there blew us away with their knowledge and acceptance of the Marriott culture. In fact, in this particular hotel, all the staff spent each day working on one of the 20 basics that define the Marriott culture. It was impressive.

War on Waste Innovation

Everyone was on the same page. The CEO saw that and knew that his goal of a changed culture was possible.

So we met with the managers and supervisors and came up with our own characteristics of the company's culture and then we defined what we called the "20 Basics." This was a mimic of the Marriott 20 Basics with the company's own items. Every morning or at the beginning of every shift, one of the 20 Basics was reviewed by the shift foreman and his supervisors with small groups to get the proper attention. When each of the 20 basics was covered the first time, the 20 were repeated again and again. After all, these 20 basics were important. Each person was given a little card (business card size with 3 folds and embossed). It was also printed in Spanish for the large Mexican employee population. It became very important to all the employees. You could ask each employee what Basic was covered on any day and most could respond correctly. It is still in effect and positive 8 years later.

The imperative to change at this company was driven by the fact that the CEO had his agenda and his new manager had his own agenda that was not in sync with the CEO's agenda. He wanted to establish his own management style and control the culture of the company. In the War on Waste, the CEO is in charge of defining the culture of the company and defining and managing strategy. There was no specific written description of the company culture. So a culture needed to be defined. And it was.

All CEOs have to guide their companies along this thin path at the edge of chaos. It isn't an easy path to follow. There are many obstructions that can throw a company into chaos. When these challenges arise, the CEO needs to be ready to move. In the case of the CEO above, I am reporting this as the problem is unfolding. It is a work in process. And it will work

Leonard Bertain, Ph.D.

because I have faith in this guy. He is a survivor. He has fallen off the edge of chaos into the abyss before. All good CEOs will find themselves in the abyss at one time or another and the good ones will find their way out.

Miscellaneous

Leonard Bertain, Ph.D.

Hubris Meter

Hubris is defined as unjustified arrogance. I am not sure whether there is any time that justifies arrogance but we can live with that definition.

I noticed a number of years ago that an owner of a business began to strut the walk of hubris because of what he had accomplished in his business. And then evil things happened to him. He lost three big orders in a row and had to lay off personnel as a result. Something had happened and I noticed similar occurrences with other clients. In fact, these same things happened to me. I would get arrogant about some accomplishment and bad things would happen. A project that I expected to get would fall through. And so forth.

So I figured out that there must be a God of Hubris. He stands in the heavens with his "Hubris Meter" and is continually searching the world for those whose "Hubris" indicator has passed some unknown level. When the Hubris Indicator goes off, the victim suffers big time as a result.

Although I am joking here, there is a certain level of truth to the old adage, "be careful of who you step on going up the success ladder because you never know who you may need on your way down."

When I mention this to my clients and my business friends they all laugh not because it is nonsense but there is a certain level of truth to this. All of them have fallen victim to the sin of hubris and they all felt that they were victims of the God of Hubris' wrath at some time.

My message is this: enjoy your success but don't become arrogant. Your clients and prospective clients will sense hubris.

War on Waste Innovation

Trade Show Rationale

A number of years ago, I managed some engineers and could never get them to deliver products on time. I was desperate to get them to deliver a product to meet a schedule that was good for the shareholders. The engineers could care less.

Then I had a bright idea. I went to the engineering team and told them that if they got the product done on time that the whole team (all 6 of the them) could go to a trade show in New Orleans to make the product announcement. They got excited and because the trade show was two weeks before the targeted delivery, the product was ready on time.

So when you look at the training of engineers, how did they get A's on their report cards. They did their homework assignments each week and got A's on the tests. But they were trained over 4 years of college or university work to know that if you didn't get your problem set in on time that you were in trouble. And most engineers look at the assignment to get the product development complete for the tradeshow as just another deadline like a homework assignment. And they get the assignment done. But if you ask them to get it done to meet corporate profit objectives they could care less.

That is not an accident. Think about it. How do we ever get anything done? We have a deadline that we "believe" is critical. In my private life, I know that if I want to get a patio finished I will encourage my wife (or maybe she just manages me the same way that I managed the engineers) to have a party. The patio gets finished. It happens all the time. So after all these years, I know that if I want to get something done, I set an artificial deadline and then work everyone involved to get the deadline completed.

Leonard Bertain, Ph.D.

But the engineers and trade shows is very interesting. I went to Comdex in Las Vegas 25 years ago and asked about 20 CEOs exhibiting new products at the show "would any of the products that you are showing today have been completed without the deadline of the Comdex trade show?" In every case, the answer was no. The tradeshow made it happen.

So my conclusion is this, if you want to get a product completed on time, find a trade show that is in a city that the engineers wants to go to. Make this trade show about 2 weeks before the product really needs to be done and make that a target for the engineering team. The new product will get done in time for the targeted delivery." I rest my case. It works.

A Final Thought

When we talk to people at the various clients that we have had over the years, a single issue emerged. We continually asked what is it that Managers want, employees want, customers want, suppliers want and unions want? What is it that all of us want. And it was a big revelation to me when it dawned on me.

We all want respect and clarity.

With respect we are dealing with the most fundamental of human needs. We made sure that the War on Waste delivered "earned" respect to all participants. Respect is a one-way street but "earned" respect is the premium in that it requires both parties in the process to contribute positively to the exchange. We employ the term "earned" respect because it is not an acknowledgement that is freely bestowed. It is "earned." And that is critical here.

We hope that the reader will try to understand the complex nature of running an organization and how lost most employees get in the bowels of any company. So when CEOs initiate an energy initiative or any activity that allows employees to gain "earned respect" they are doing a great service in spite of all the difficulties that I have pointed out. The effort will be worth it.

As for clarity, what more can I say. We live in a world of obfuscation. Nothing is what it seems: sales promotions bait and switch; raises are gobbled up by the cost of living; employees live the Tribal Knowledge Paradox; and on and on it goes. So when CEOs communicate to employees, I urge simplicity and above all clarity.
